Kidnap

From The Case Files of

Claire Welch

Contents

Introduction

In June 1933, a threat to kidnap Sarah Delano Roosevelt, the baby granddaughter of the US President, from the summer home of her parents, James Roosevelt and Betsey Cushing Roosevelt, was reported in the *Boston Post*. Although shocking news, in the early half of the 20th century, kidnapping was fast becoming a real threat.

The Roosevelt's New Hampshire home was partially destroyed by fire on 15th June and a Secret Service agent was detailed to guard the child, although the President, Franklin Delano Roosevelt (FDR as he was also known), denied the *Post*'s report. The terror of kidnap gangs in the United States had led to a number of the country's richest parents sending their children abroad in order to keep them safe, and a special identification system was introduced in schools to foil would-be kidnappers. By the early 1930s, the death penalty was strongly advocated as a suitable punishment for this heinous crime. The most notorious case in the early part of the decade was that of the Lindbergh baby in 1932. For 72 days the world was scoured for clues as to the toddler's whereabouts and Colonel Lindbergh paid £10,000 to a gang who purported to be able to return the child. The boy's body was found in early May 1932, hidden under a pile of leaves in a wood near his parents' estate at Hopewell, New Jersey. Several arrests were made, but no convictions were brought and affluent Americans began to panic for the safety of their own children. They were right to be afraid. In the month before reports of the threat to Sarah Delano Roosevelt were known, Judge McElroy, city manager of Kansas City, paid £6,000 to kidnappers for the safe return of his daughter, Mary McElroy. Children of wealthy Americans were not the only ones under threat. In February 1933 in Denver, Charles Boettcher, a close friend of Lindbergh, was kidnapped in front of his wife, who was handed a ransom note demanding $60,000, as two armed men bundled her husband into a small sedan. She was also told not to contact the police and to remember what had happened to baby Lindbergh, whom the kidnappers warned would have been safely returned to his family had the ransom been paid more promptly. Around the same time, pilot and navigator Harold Gatty and his wife, along with film star Bebe Daniels, were among others who received threats. In the early 1930s, the American kidnapping rackets brought about the existence of a "criminal parasite" known as a "chiseller". The chiseller attempted to obtain money from the victims of the kidnapping by posing as the kidnapper. Then there are the victims who choose to stay with their kidnappers...

In January 2007, after decades of kidnapping on both sides of the Atlantic, an article in the *Daily Mirror* highlighted the cases of those victims who actively agreed to stay with the people who had taken them from the security of their lives. It begins: "It is the greatest puzzle in a baffling case... why didn't Shawn Hornbeck try to escape?" Snatched at the age of 11 and held captive for four years, the child apparently had plenty of chances to get away from his kidnapper, Michael Devlin. He was allowed sleepovers with friends, was given a mobile phone and was even spoken to by police who suspected him of skipping school, yet he stayed...

In 2006, Austrian schoolgirl Natascha Kampusch grieved for the man who had held her prisoner for eight years. It emerged that, like Shawn, she had rejected several opportunities to flee her own kidnapper, Wolfgang Priklopil. Shawn and Natascha were both victims of what is now recognized as Stockholm Syndrome, in which a kidnap victim or hostage forms a bond with their captor. Forensic psychologist Dr Glenn Wilson says that an unexpected reversal of loyalties can occur as a result of a survival mechanism during a period of extreme stress and danger. "You're totally dependent on your captor – whether you live or die, eat or starve – and everything is channelled through them", he states. "You develop an intense dependency on them, which becomes a friendship or even love – albeit a perverted kind", says Wilson. The term Stockholm Syndrome was first coined by criminologist Nils Bejerot to explain events during a bank robbery that went wrong in the Swedish capital in 1973. Raiders Jan-Erik Olsson and Clark Olofsson held four hostages during a six-day stand-off with police. The first sign that loyalties were switching came when hostage Kristin Ehnemark told police negotiators that she and the other hostages were "relaxed" with the criminals – but concerned that they could be hurt in any rescue attempt. Even when the robbers attached snares around the necks of their prisoners to prevent rescue, the hostages continued to side with the criminals. When the siege ended peacefully, Olofsson and Ehnemark became lifelong friends. In an even more extreme example, American newspaper heiress Patty Hearst joined the terrorist Symbionese Liberation Army (SLA) that had abducted her – and eventually went with them on subsequent bank raids. Dr Wilson said that the bonding between captor and captive can be intense. "Natascha Kampusch apparently bonded with her captor to the point where she felt sad when he killed himself", he said. "It begins with people trying to befriend their captors so they will be treated better. And very often the captors operate a kind of propaganda. They'll say things like, 'Your parents don't care for you', or 'You've been abandoned by the rest of the world'", he explained. Wilson goes on to say, "And if there's sexual gratification there too, it would increase the bonding."

Estate agent Stephanie Slater was kidnapped by murderer Michael Sams while showing him around a house in Birmingham in 1992. Now 40 and living on the Isle of Wight, she told the *Mirror*, "I was blindfolded, gagged, kept in a tiny coffin for eight days and on my first night he raped me. But I built up a rapport with him in order to save my life. I talked to him so that he wouldn't kill me. He started to enjoy talking to me, which meant he didn't put me in the box for as long." The article goes on to explain how Stephanie thought that Shawn Hornbeck may have been forced to use similar tactics. "He would have depended on his captor for food, drink, everything, even going to the toilet", she said. "The kidnapper becomes the person you rely on, so a relationship develops." But it is often a relationship reinforced by violence. The same can be said of those in abusive relationships, who have been effectively "groomed" to believe that the only person who can help them survive the situation they're in – and the only one on whom they can depend – is the one person who has put them in an intolerable position in the first place, their abuser. Wilson continues: "It can begin with periods of sadism, coercion and total domination and so when they progress to granting favours and kindness the victim is more receptive." Patty Hearst's recruitment into the SLA is a classic example. The anarchists kidnapped her in 1974 and held her captive for 18 months, during which time she was raped, tortured and brainwashed about the evils of capitalism. "I was blindfolded, gagged and tied", she said years later. "I was deprived of sight, light, sleep and food." But, when the nightmare ended, Patty joined them.

It appears that a number of kidnap victims need to build rapport with their captors in order to fight for their survival. They know they are dependent on the person holding them for absolutely everything and they form a "relationship" in the hope of better treatment and a chance to save their own lives. It may be quite shocking to those who have never been through the ordeal, but this instinctive tactic makes perfect sense when you consider just how desperate and in despair kidnap victims must feel. However, there are many more issues that could, and should, be pursued before all those who have experienced this heinous crime are lumped together in terms of their responses to their individual situations.

This book takes a look at some notorious kidnappings, touching on the cases that have blighted society for the past 100 years. While it was generally accepted that kidnap involved the removal of a person (or persons) against their will, holding them with the promise of their safe return if a ransom was paid, today kidnap seems to have a much broader meaning. In the US, it was usual for a ransom to be paid after a person had been kidnapped. However, with abductions on the increase, the term "kidnap" became extended to include the taking of children by men, women and gangs, either for sexual gratification or other purposes, including selling them for high financial gain.

Kidnap is a chilling reminder of the power that people can, and do, exert over others, particularly the vulnerable and the young. Kidnapping for money is still a common occurrence in many parts of the world today. Places such as Mexico and Colombia have been described as the "kidnapping capitals of the world". This dubious honour is now held by Iraq. Places of conflict, alongside impoverished areas of the globe, have seen kidnapping on the increase; militias, organized crime and drug trafficking (for which kidnapping is part of solving unpaid debt issues) also contribute to this crime.

Kidnapping is also prevalent in some parts of the world as a means for obtaining slaves, and human trafficking is reported to be the fastest growing criminal industry across the globe. These forms of kidnap see profits of billions of dollars for the perpetrators. Often, those kidnapped by traffickers, particularly women and children, are subjected to a life of sexual exploitation. Victims of these crimes are usually impoverished and living in extreme circumstances at the time they are kidnapped. They are also less likely to be missed by loving families and friends. Tourists are also prone to becoming victims of crimes involving kidnap, particularly in cities and other areas where organized crime prevails and ransoms are thought to be easy money. However, kidnap victims come from all ethnic and social backgrounds. At this point in time, the International Labour Organization estimates that around 250 million children between the ages of 5 and 17 are being exploited after being "forcibly removed" from their families. In the UK, just as elsewhere in the world, paedophile rings take and use children for their own sexual gratification, violence and control. Often, these children do not survive the kidnap. The word paedophile literally means "lover of children". Writing in the *Daily Mirror* in July 2000 after the disappearance of Sarah Payne, columnist Brian Reade (who had a 6-year-old daughter of his own) asked: "Is there any other word in our language so ill-defined?" Ultimately, there was a terrible gut-wrenching inevitability about the final few days of Sarah Payne's life. Brian Reade writes:

"It started with a wry smile of recognition when you hear a 'Right Little Miss' has stomped off after a tiff with her brothers and sister. It turns to fear when her bed is unslept in for a night. Then there is a surge of hope as optimistic possibilities flood the brain. She could be in hiding. She may have had an accident and we will find her. Someone may have led her astray, seen the light, and returned her unharmed."

There are many more parents who have probably felt those same feelings or had those same thoughts. However, sadly, the despicable killing of young children has been part of society for many years. Brian Reade wanted to know in 2000 what society could do to stop it.

Jamie Lavis, 8, was kidnapped and murdered in May 1997 by paedophile bus driver Darren Vickers, who sexually abused the small boy, killed him and dismembered his body. Katrina Monk, 12, was killed in May 1993 by 24-year-old neighbour Keith Collard, who kidnapped her at gunpoint and forced her into his garden shed in Enfield, London. Her body was found the following day in nettles, with a plastic bag taped over her head. She had been sexually assaulted. In 1994 Timothy Morss and Brett Tyler took 9-year-old Daniel Handley from the streets of Beckton, east London, where the child was playing and subjected him to a fearsome sex attack – which they recorded on video – before killing the boy and burying him on a golf course. Jason Swift, 14, had run away from home but was snatched by Sidney Cooke in 1984. The ex-fairground worker led the gang jailed for strangling the boy, who was later found in a shallow grave. Cooke was also named by a fellow paedophile as the man who snatched and killed Mark Tildesley, age 7, whose body has never been found. Cooke was never prosecuted for the crime. Six-year-old Barry Lewis was also murdered by Sidney Cooke's gang during a homosexual orgy. The youngster from New Cross, south London, was thought to be among nine boys killed by the paedophile ring in the 1980s.

Susan Blatchford, 11, was one of two "babes in the wood" killed by Ronald Jebson. She vanished in March 1970 while walking near her home in Enfield, north London. Jebson gave her drugs, sexually assaulted her and then strangled her. Twelve-year-old Gary Hanlon was the second of the "babes in the wood" killed by Jebson. Rosemary Papper, 8, was raped and murdered by Jebson in 1974. He had been lodging with her parents but vowed to "get them" after a row. The next day, he picked up Rosemary from school and abused her. He then drove her around for three hours before strangling her. Nine-year-old Laura Kane was raped and murdered by a family friend, Colin Bainbridge, in 1999. He lured her to his home in Murton, Co Durham, attacked her and hid her body under the floorboards. Hours later he went for a drink with her mum, Carol, and comforted her as a 10-day search continued for the child. In 1982, 11-year-old Susan Maxwell, allowed to walk home for the first time on her own, was snatched near the farmhouse where she lived at Cornhill-on-Tweed, Northumberland by Robert Black. Five-year-old Caroline Hogg was also a victim of Robert Black. He picked her up outside her home in Portobello, near Edinburgh. He took her to a funfair, paid for a ride on a roundabout and then took her by the hand to lead her to her death. Black was also responsible for kidnapping 10-year-old Sarah Harper while she was on her way to a local shop for a loaf of bread. Trucker Black drove her from Leeds and dumped her body in the Midlands. All three (of his then known victims) were found along roads he used on his deliveries.

Twelve-year-old Thomas Marshall was strangled with his own necklace and his body dumped 50 miles from his home. Killer, Kevan Roberts, had feared that the boy would expose his gay affair with a married cousin. Roberts was caught when police found a bead from the boy's chain in the U-bend of his sink. Rosie Palmer was just 3 years old when she was abducted, sexually abused and murdered by Shaun Armstrong. He had lured the small girl after buying her an ice cream. Her battered body was found in a cupboard. In 1995 Sophie Hook, 7, was raped and strangled by depraved Howard Hughes after she was snatched from a tent in her uncle's garden in Llandudno, North Wales. While on Boxing Day 1992, the body of 14-year-old Johanna Young was discovered in a frozen pond. She died from drowning but had a fractured skull. Her murder has never been solved.

There is a never a happy ending to these stories when children take centre stage in a kidnap or abduction. As Brian Reade writes:

"Never when they die an unimaginably vile death at the hands of what is sadly almost surely a paedophile. We have learned over the years a brutal truth. When paedophiles steal innocence they never give it back. They consume it. Like buzzards around a corpse, it is what they feed on... It is why, without question, they are the lowest of the lowest forms of life on earth. These people do not 'love' children. It is about power and violation... They physically and mentally rip children to pieces because they despise their innocence. They are sadists pure and simple. They are inflicted with an incurable disease, the most terrifying disease there is, and it is in this light that society should view the severity of their threat. But we fail to meet their evil head-on at our peril...

"By allowing paedophile rings to flourish on the internet, in magazines, in the midst of our community, we are laying the seeds for the next Sarah Payne. By handing down light sentences which insult the memory of every Sarah Payne, who was unable to walk safely through a field on a summer's day without being subjected to the worst form of depravity, we let down every child in the land. By releasing known violent paedophiles back into the community unwatched, we dice with death.

"If you want to see how trivially we take their threat look at the way we treated Gary Glitter. Here was a man found with a mountain of the most sickening child pornography on his computer which he had downloaded for his own pleasure, and what do we do? We give him a few months prison, then let him out after a matter of weeks because he was allegedly receiving death threats. He is then released to stand before cameras and weep tears of self-pity, without one ounce of remorse for the child victims he used to get his kicks."

Gary Glitter made the headlines again in 2012, along with Freddie Starr, when investigations took place over the alleged abuse carried out over 40 years by the late Jimmy Saville on so many young victims. Once again, Glitter was questioned by police over his alleged abuse of children during the time he and Saville were celebrities during the latter decades of the 20th century.

Talking of the pain that Michael Payne, Sarah's father, showed after his daughter was found brutally murdered, Brian Reade concluded: "He will relive the worst of the horrors that may or may not have happened. He will never think straight or smile genuinely again. He has just been visited by the worst nightmare that can ever visit a father. And he is a broken man. Let us not let his image fade." Michael Payne, like the parents of the other kidnap and murder victims in this book, and those who were kidnapped and survived their horrendous ordeals, should all be remembered for the utter horror, fear and terror that the perpetrators of this heinous crime have put them through. As Brian Reade puts it: "Let us not betray the children any longer."

Marion Parker

(1927)

William Edward Hickman, aged 17, found himself in jail, heavily guarded, in Pendleton, Oregon, in the United States in December 1927. Hickman was charged with the kidnap and murder of a 12-year-old schoolgirl from Los Angeles, Marion Parker. After Hickman's arrest in Oregon, officials awaited extradition papers following a special session of the grand jury that had indicted the young man. The extradition papers were hurried through and two detectives travelled to Pendleton to serve warrants on Hickman, who was known as "The Fox". After gruelling questioning by police, he confessed to the murder and dismemberment of Marion Parker's body. Previously, he had alleged that drug fiend Andrew Kramer, a name made famous in a Whitechapel murder in London in 1881, was the true kidnapper and murderer of the young girl. However, Kramer had been found guilty of the London crime and had cheated the gallows by plunging to his death in the River Thames. A bank clerk and student of criminal history, Hickman had been studying the circumstances of the 1881 murder, and it was found that the details of the earlier crime matched those surrounding Marion's death.

The young girl was taken from Los Angeles where she lived and was murdered, despite her father paying a £300 ransom. Hickman was sentenced to death by hanging when he was convicted for the crime at a trial in Los Angeles, but he was again charged with murder in February 1928 when he was accused, along with Welby Hunt, of killing shop assistant Ivy Tombs in a hold-up at the store where the young woman worked.

Hickman's kidnap and murder of Marion Parker was described by the press at the time as "the most horrible crime of the 1920s". Why he actually took Marion has caused speculation. Did he need the money? Was he crazy? Or, was this a revenge attack against a former employer? Perry Parker, Marion's father, was a prominent Los Angeles banker who had been called to give evidence in a trial against Hickman for the theft and fraud of cheques. Hickman was sent to prison for the crime. Whether it was this that motivated the young bank clerk is hard to prove, but Hickman had arrived at Mount Vernon Junior High School, telling the school registrar, Mary Holt, that Perry Parker had been badly injured in an accident at work and that he wanted to see his daughter. What Hickman did not know was that there were two Parker girls; Marion had a twin sister, Marjorie. However, the would-be kidnapper was so convincing posing as an employee of Mr Parker, and so disarming, that Holt believed his story and brought Marion to reception, where she asked her to accompany the stranger so that she could see her "injured" father.

Having kidnapped Marion, Hickman sent ransom letters to Parker for several days, signing himself off with "The Fox", "Death" and "Fate". The search for Marion during this time involved more than 20,000 police officers and American Legion volunteers. A reward was offered but no new information came to light, until it was suggested that the kidnapper was someone with a grudge against Perry Parker – and suspicion fell on Hickman.

Parker failed in his first attempt to deliver a ransom to Hickman when the criminal saw police in the drop-off area. Eventually, a rendezvous was arranged on the corner of Fifth Avenue and South Manhattan Street in Los Angeles and Perry Parker handed over £300 to a man waiting in a parked car. Marion was seated next to the man in the passenger seat. It appeared that she was wrapped tightly to her neck and unable to move. As soon as Hickman had the money, he drove off and pushed the girl out of the car towards the end of the street. It transpired that Marion had been dead for about 12 hours and her body had already been dismembered, but Hickman, fearing he wouldn't receive the ransom for a dead child, had hastily wrapped Marion's body in order to fool her father into believing his daughter was still alive. Marion's arms and legs had been severed from her body (they were found on 18th December 1927 wrapped in newspaper) and she had been disembowelled and stuffed with a towel, to soak up the blood. Her eyes had been wired open to give the appearance of life. Under questioning, Hickman described how he had strangled Marion and cut her throat, although he believed she was still alive when he began to dismember her. Hickman alleged to the police that he had never intended to kill the young girl, but had felt he had no choice once she learned his identity and that he had previously worked for her father. He had tried to claim he was insane, but this was quickly dismissed by the jury and court officials, when prison guards testified that prior to his trial Hickman had asked how to appear crazy. Despite having disposed of Marion's body and body parts, and the car in which he collected the ransom, Hickman was eventually linked to the crime by fingerprint analysis from his earlier crimes (including armed robbery), which matched those on the ransom letters and the car, which was later recovered by police.

Hickman fled to Oregon but was recognized on "Wanted" posters. He was extradited back to Los Angeles, tried and executed in San Quentin prison in October 1928, having failed to convince the jury that he was insane. He was one of the first criminals to argue his defence by using a new law introduced by California allowing pleas of not guilty by reason of insanity.

Charles Lindbergh Jr

(1932)

On 3rd March 1932, a small bed in the nursery of a New Jersey country house lay empty and the United States waited anxiously for news of Atlantic pilot Colonel Lindbergh's baby son, who had been kidnapped the previous day. The kidnapping sparked an intensive hunt for the baby who was being held for a £10,000 ransom. The search included troops and police from three states, as well as Canadian border officials and 200 further police who were detailed to comb New York State. Rewards (including £2,000 from the state of New Jersey) were offered to those willing to come forward with information leading to the arrest of the kidnappers, and President Hoover conferred with the US Attorney General whom he had summoned on hearing the news, to help bring the baby home safely. Lindbergh and other noted pilots, including Admiral Byrd and Clarence D Chamberlin, searched the countryside in planes, and the Federal Department of Justice in Washington placed their services at the disposal of the searchers. Lindbergh was ready and willing to pay the ransom demanded and early on in the investigation received a postcard, which read: "Baby safe, instructions later. Act accordingly". It followed the ransom note that had been found on the windowsill of the nursery, which threatened harm to the child if the £10,000 was not paid.

The kidnapping of 20-month-old Charles Lindbergh brought

about national anger, following two years of a wave of kidnappings for ransom in which more than 2,000 people had been abducted. Described as a "racket", it was becoming increasingly obvious that kidnapping, alongside robbery, vice, and drugs and liquor was worth "big money". After the first night of searching for the Lindbergh's baby, the police re-enacted the abduction in order to gain a better perspective on the events surrounding the child's disappearance. His mother, Anne Morrow Lindbergh, was stated in the press to have spent the entire time crying at the loss of her son. The police raised the rough makeshift ladder used by the kidnappers to the nursery windowsill on which they had already discovered muddy boot marks. The shutter was warped and had refused to close when the baby was put to bed, which left the kidnappers with an easy entrance. While a fingerprint expert examined the sill, New York's Chief of Police, Mulrooney, described the kidnapping as "most vicious" and ordered the police to co-operate with New Jersey forces. In the congested areas of New York County, the search included combing hospitals and nurseries where babies received medical treatment, as well as homes where newly established occupants had recently arrived with babies. Every entry and exit to New York was closely guarded and the general belief at the time was that the kidnappers may have tried to reach Canada. Within a few hours of the news breaking of the abduction, 300 cars had been stopped before being permitted to cross the Peace Bridge. It was at this point that Lindbergh's fraternity, known as the "Bird-Men", took to the sky in an attempt to form an aerial posse to aid the search for Charles.

The first clue in the case was provided by highway workmen at Princeton who, shortly before the baby went missing, reported that they had been approached for directions to the Lindbergh estate by two men in a dark sedan. However, Captain John Lamb of the New York State Police believed that the kidnapping was the work of an "abnormal person" and decided to question staff and residents of a nearby home for epileptics. Charles Lindbergh, however, was not the only child to go missing at this time. On 3rd March, 11-year-old James de Jute, the son of a wealthy contractor, was seized and bundled into a car on his way to school in Niles, Ohio.

The following day, seemingly laughing in the face of the family of their victim and the authorities, the kidnappers sent a disturbing letter to Colonel Lindbergh that stated: "Read this and keep your mouth closed". The letter began with:

"Don't open your trap to a living soul. If you do, it will be your last tale. Your father has plenty of money. So do as you are instructed. If you do, no harm will come to you. But you remember the fate of the Smith girl, who received a similar letter and then did contrary to our instructions by making it known to her father and friends. She dropped out of the picture. So will you if you tell anybody about the contents of this letter."

It continued: "We want fifty thousand dollars and we will forward our instructions for the delivery of the same. Do not set a trap or the price will be higher and the penalty severe."

Frances W Smith, mentioned in the letter to Lindbergh,

disappeared on 13th January 1928 from Smith College. Her body was later found in the Connecticut River. The letter, delivered on 4th March 1932, followed Lindbergh's announcement that he intended to fight it out with the kidnappers. Meanwhile, four men and a boy were being questioned by police. A further letter was posted in Boston by a woman – who urged it to be delivered to Lindbergh immediately and then sped off in a car. The letter, which was believed by police to be genuine, read: "Dear Colonel Lindbergh – I do not wish to say how the following information came into my possession, but I urge you to act upon it. I know that your son is held by two men and a woman at Provincetown, N.J. I have received this information from a long-distance call."

Meanwhile, the press revealed the contents of the ransom note found at the scene of the baby's disappearance, which threatened death to the child if its contents were published. Al Capone, Chicago's leading gangster (who was in Leavenworth prison at the time), was indignant over the kidnapping and from his cell offered a reward of £2,000 for information leading to the recovery of the child unharmed and the capture of his captors. "It is the most outrageous thing I have heard of", Capone stormed, adding, "If I were out of jail I could be of real assistance." Police then permitted the publication of a report in which they inferred that the baby was being held in a house not far from Hopewell and the family's estate.

The story dominated the newspapers in the days after the child was taken and, in a heartbroken appeal on 4th March 1932, Anne Morrow Lindbergh gave her pledge that the kidnappers would be granted immunity if they returned her son. "Colonel Lindbergh and I want to make personal contact with the kidnappers of our child", she stated. Mrs Lindbergh continued: "Our only interest is his safe and immediate return." It was also known to the public by this time that the £10,000 ransom was sanctioned for immediate dispatch. Developments began to take place in the UK too, when police inquiries led to the arrest of two men. Back in the US, a letter was given to the police by postal workers. The letter read: "Your baby is safe. Put 50,000 dollars as shown in the accompanying diagram. We are on the look-out and if anything goes wrong the kid will be killed. We are not fooling." Unfortunately, the police were unable to decipher the diagram. On the same day, two further men were arrested in connection with the case. Patsy Mucciola – whose real name was believed to be Patsy Orlondo – left Hopewell on the night of the kidnapping and Henry (Red) Johnson, the chauffeur, who was reported to be the sweetheart of the baby's 23-year-old nurse, Betty Gow, from Glasgow. Charles Lindbergh's nurse was also questioned for several hours but was found to have no connection with the kidnapping.

On 6th March, news came from New York that the Lindbergh baby was safe and would be returned within 48 hours. Johnson remained in police custody while the Lindberghs gave their consent for racketeers Salvy Spitale and Irving Bitz to act as mediators with the kidnappers, after an ultimatum issued by the underworld to the abductors threatening vengeance and a note from the perpetrators themselves stating they preferred to deal with someone with underworld influence. A committee of leading gangsters issued the following warning to the kidnappers: "Return the child. Accept ransom within twenty-four hours or you're through." They also pledged to support Spitale and Bitz. However, this involvement of two of the underworld's "kings" came as a shock to the public. Spitale – known as "the fixer" – and his trusted lieutenant, Bitz – were widely reported to have been involved in the shooting of Jack "Legs" Diamond in October 1930 and his subsequent assassination. The legal authorities sided with the Lindberghs and declared that both men would be given legal immunity while they carried out their own investigations into the baby's kidnapping. Meanwhile, Scotland Yard became involved in the case when two men from the UK, each with dubious pasts, were known to have moved to the US. As a result, several phone calls were made by the Yard to the Connecticut State Attorney. Johnson was moved to Newark, still under arrest, while the suggestion was made that the baby's hair could have been dyed or greased in order to hide his curly golden hair.

Many officials gave their opinions on the case, including the governor of Sing Sing Prison, who said: "I do not believe the kidnapping was the work of the underworld, nor do the inmates here. Professionals would have asked for more money." The governor added that all the inmates of Sing Sing were resentful at the affair as a slur upon them as "professionals". By now the case was described as causing "excitement" across America to the exclusion of all other news topics. With no attempts by the kidnappers to secure the ransom money, troopers, police and detectives continued to scour the countryside for miles around the Lindbergh home in the hope of finding some evidence as to the baby's whereabouts. While the Lindberghs may have been convinced of an underworld involvement in the kidnapping of their son, the authorities were equally convinced that the kidnappers were amateurs.

By 8th March 1932, Governor Moore of New Jersey, a close friend of Colonel Lindbergh declared that: "We have no tangible evidence that the Lindbergh baby is alive. I am powerless to promise the kidnappers immunity – even if Colonel Lindbergh asked me to. My idea is to put every resource of the State and the nation into the case. The Secret Service is at work throughout the country." Meanwhile, Johnson's associate provided him with an alibi and he was released by Newark police. Spitale and Bitz still hadn't managed to make contact with the kidnappers and were working secretly and independently of all others involved by this stage. A further letter, written in red ink and unsigned, demanding $50,000 (£10,000) was intercepted by police and regarded as a hoax. The speculation surrounding the baby's kidnap continued unabated and those of notable popularity, particularly in Hollywood, were scared for their own children. Many homes of the rich and famous were put under guard by private detectives. During the early hours of 9th March, while Colonel Lindbergh's household was asleep, he met with a mysterious visitor, said to be an emissary of his baby's kidnappers. About an hour before dawn, the Colonel sent his car to Princeton railroad station and state troopers in the district were instructed to let the car pass without question and not to try and identify the vehicle's occupants. The visitor, a man, had phoned Lindbergh before making his visit. It was reported in the *Daily Mirror* that the ceaseless activity of the police in holding up letters and telegrams and listening to phone calls was causing increasing annoyance for the Lindbergh family. They felt that the police investigation was so thorough in its approach that it was causing frustration on both sides, and so the governor of New Jersey had promised that the police would no longer open mail sent to the Lindbergh address. The day after Colonel Lindbergh's meeting with the mysterious visitor, a new development in the search for the kidnapped baby was reported from Cumberland, West Virginia, when troopers stated that they had begun a hurried search in the wild Tygart Valley region after an unknown motorist handed a pedestrian a scrawled note reading: "Baby alive 32 miles south of Elkins (West Virginia). Lindbergh baby in log cabin alone without food." Meanwhile, it was believed that secret negotiations were under way and that the baby would be back home before long. Other reports stated that Charles Lindbergh was on a boat and that the Colonel had known for several days where his son was being kept. On the ninth day of the search it was revealed that Spitale's wife had received threats of kidnap against her own two children should her husband not end his efforts to find the missing baby. It was clear that not all members of the underworld supported the Lindberghs. Meanwhile, 6,000 travellers were asked to join the search by their chiefs. The rumours continued, including those that claimed Lindbergh was dressing in uniforms and disguises in order to search anonymously for his abducted son. The first real breakthrough was thought to have occurred on 12th March when the *Detroit News* quoted Isaiah Leebove, said to be the attorney to Spitale, who said that he had received information that the baby was safe, but that a ransom of much more than £10,000 was wanted. Meanwhile, at 1am that same day, Claude Anderson, a wealthy artist, heard a noise coming from his child's nursery and found his baby in the arms of a strange man. After a desperate struggle in the dark, the would-be kidnapper escaped from the house in Riverton, New Jersey. By day 12 of the search for baby Charles all clues seemed to lead to nowhere and nothing had been discovered that would bring the case to an end.

On 16th March, two weeks into the investigation, for the first time police disclosed their misgivings with regard to the possible fate of the child. Fears were revealed that the baby was dead when it became known that the police had circularized all keepers of incinerators in hotels, apartment blocks and city institutions to watch for any parcels containing baby clothes. Colonel and Mrs Lindbergh did not share police views that their son was dead. One woman who thought she knew the answer as to what had happened to Charles Lindbergh Jr was Leandro Lightfoot of New Brunswick, who employed a German couple. Lightfoot told the police that the night the child went missing her employees had asked to borrow her car. She subsequently discovered that they had driven it around 60 miles and the tyres were muddy. They gave their notice two days later, claiming they were returning to Germany.

After their departure, Lightfoot discovered that a crate and chisel had gone missing from her garage; a similar chisel was found at the Lindbergh home. The speculation didn't stop there, however. Four rival New York gangs bargained for the return of the baby: two claimed they actually knew his whereabouts while the other two were merely angling to cheat his parents out of the ransom money. Governor Moore, meanwhile, claimed on day 19 that an abandoned car, buried in hay in a barn near Hopewell, New Jersey, was the most promising clue yet, while three men were arrested as part of a gang of car thieves. Charles Lindbergh was then apparently spotted being taken in a car through Juarez, Mexico, while in Europe, a professor taking his own child to hospital – who closely resembled the Lindbergh child – was almost lynched by an angry mob who mistook his son for the missing baby. Tensions were running high and almost reached fever pitch at the end of March 1932 when Dr Dobson-Peacock, a Virginia clergyman (acting as an intermediary), claimed he had seen the child on board a yacht run by rum-runners. Two other emissaries acting for Colonel Lindbergh, Admiral Burrage and a J H Curtis, were also approached by the rum-runners and it was widely believed by this time that the child was somewhere off the Virginia or Maryland coast.

Dr Dobson-Peacock left Norfolk, Virginia, urgently on 29th March 1932 to visit the Lindberghs. It was reported in the newspapers that he had positive means for identifying the baby, plans for having him returned home and details about the ransom demands. Curtis was believed to have been in direct contact with the kidnappers, with all that remained being to agree the terms of the ransom. All three emissaries, it was believed, were then to take a chartered boat to meet with the kidnappers who were reportedly hiding on a vessel outside the 12-mile limit. It was the latest in a long line of theories, which like the others would come to nothing. The next news came a month after baby Lindbergh was first kidnapped when Major Schoeffel, assistant to Colonel Schwarzkopf, head of the New Jersey police, was known to have set sail for Europe in connection with the case, bound for Scotland Yard. He docked at Southampton in early April 1932 amidst secrecy. His passport was unchecked, his name didn't appear on the passenger list and his cabin was vacated an hour before the liner reached Plymouth. He seemingly had no baggage and there was no trace of him boarding the boat train to London's Waterloo station. However, there was a message for him on the platform which read: "Message for Major Schoeffel. Apply at gate." He travelled to London by road and all press attempts to interview him failed. He met with heads of CID at Scotland Yard and was believed to be heading for Glasgow (the home town of Betty Gow, the nursery nurse of Charles Lindbergh). On 7th April 1932, Curtis announced to the press that contact had been made with the kidnappers and that the Lindbergh baby was well. Meanwhile, the police rushed to a point in Waquoit Bay, off the Massachusetts coast, following a report that a man, woman and baby had been seen in a boat heading for Great Neck. On 11th April, in a formal statement issued by Colonel Schwarzkopf, it was announced that Colonel Lindbergh had paid $50,000 (£10,000) to the kidnappers on the agreement that he would be notified of the whereabouts of his baby son. The kidnappers failed to keep their end of the bargain and, after waiting several days, the Colonel requested the aid of the federal government in tracing the dollar bills. Officials did not believe he had paid the money to the actual kidnappers, but to men claiming to have the baby. The Colonel had followed instructions to fly over Martha's Vineyard, off the coast of Massachusetts. The next day, following the "double crossing" by the kidnappers' agent, in accepting the ransom but not returning the baby, the situation was naturally tense. Anne Lindbergh was reported to have collapsed at the news and it was feared that with the publication of the serial numbers of the notes in which the ransom was paid, and the attempts of the Federal authorities to trace them, that the baby's life was in real danger. In a desperate attempt to rectify the situation, Colonel Lindbergh offered to change the notes for gold – and his son. The rumours, theories and arrests continued, but no tangible evidence came to light. Canadian police arrested an American man said to be carrying letters addressed to Lindbergh, while Harry Fleischer, leader of the notorious "Purple Gang" of kidnappers, was reportedly on his way to the UK where authorities were asked to arrest him upon arrival. Meanwhile, one of the ransom notes was recovered in New York. Two searches of the liner *Duchess of Atholl* were made when the vessel reached Liverpool and Salvy Spitale told newspapers that the kidnappers had received the ransom and were desperate to hand the baby back, but were still afraid of being caught. Betty Gow was formally cleared of all involvement in the case and Al Capone made a second offer to try and obtain the safe return of baby Lindbergh, should Colonel Lindbergh secure his release from prison.

More than two months after Charles Lindbergh Jr went missing, he was found dead close to his family home in Hopewell, New Jersey. An official announcement was issued on 12th May 1932 stating that the discovery of the child's body was made by neighbours of the Lindberghs. The tragic news was broken to a pregnant Anne Lindbergh at her mother's home. The body had been found almost concealed under a pile of leaves and earth. A hole about the size of a five-pence-piece was found in the skull just above the forehead and an attempt had apparently been made to bury the body. The police theory was that the baby had died some distance from Hopewell but his body had been returned by car and deposited near the estate as a crowning act of vindictiveness on the part of the disappointed murderer, or murderers.

At the time the baby went missing, Anne Lindbergh had published the child's diet in the newspapers because he was ill. It stated: "Here is a heartbroken appeal direct from the mother of the child you stole. The baby has been ill and his recovery may depend on the treatment he gets from you. You must be especially careful about his diet."

Now that there was no more harm that could come to the baby, the police set about bringing the perpetrators to justice. There was nationwide anger at the death of the little boy and, in a dramatic order to the Secret Service to assist in the investigation, President

Hoover declared that: "Efforts are never to be relaxed until the criminals are implacably brought to justice." The Colonel took a final look at his son before his cremation in mid-May 1932. He identified his son's body, following another formal identification by the baby's nurse, Betty Gow, who identified the child by his curly blonde hair, overlapping toes and eight teeth. Forensic examination of the child revealed that he had died not long after his kidnap took place, by a shot from a revolver through his head. The physician's verdict came after police findings confirmed that the baby was taken from his cot, placed in a car, brutally maltreated and then finally shot.

The brutal murder of this baby, revealed 74 days after the kidnapping, shocked the whole world. Colonel and Mrs Lindbergh were overwhelmed with messages of sympathy from all parts of the globe. Among them were messages from gang chiefs in the underworld, who reiterated their belief that the kidnapping was the work of "amateurs". Anne Morrow Lindbergh was particularly brave over the death of her son and all precautions were taken to safeguard her health in view of the fact that she was expecting to become a mother again. The greatest irony of the tragedy centred on Colonel Lindbergh. At the time the baby was found dead, he had been away from Hopewell "negotiating" with the kidnappers. Meanwhile, Curtis confessed that his so-called negotiations with the kidnappers had been false and he was arrested by New Jersey police on 18th May 1932. Curtis had been given a large sum of money to buy influence with the Norfolk (Virginia) police for a bootlegger from Long Island. Curtis didn't keep up his end of the bargain, a private detective acting for Colonel Lindbergh became suspicious of his actions and he was forced to confess to giving false reports. At the same time, his statements to the police led them to the imminent arrests of five men and a woman. Two US gangsters, a German, two Italians and one Brazilian were all believed to have been involved in the tragic case, and Curtis picked out one of the kidnappers from the police rogue gallery. However, it then came to light during hours of questioning that he'd never met any of the kidnappers. Curtis also claimed that he had been encouraged and cajoled by Dobson-Peacock to carry on the false reports long after he'd wanted to. He accused the clergyman of being "publicity mad". In June 1932, Curtis pleaded not guilty to the charge of obstructing the course of justice. Later that same month, astonishingly, Lindbergh was subpoenaed to appear as part of the defence for Curtis prior to the former shipbuilder's trial at the end of June. Meanwhile, Violet Sharpe, an Englishwoman who worked as maid to Mrs Dwight Morrow, grandmother of the murdered baby, took her own life following numerous "grilling" interviews by American police. The UK government faced questions from MPs in Parliament with regard to the woman's death, and the British acting Consul General in New York was asked to send a report of his findings back to London. In a further twist to the case, it was announced soon after that Violet Sharpe was married – as stated on her burial certificate – which came as a huge shock to the police and public alike. But, the fact that this young woman was "bullied to death", according to newspaper reports, was investigated in the House of Commons, where questions were asked.

A Secret Service agent, Gaston Means, was meanwhile found guilty of larceny of £20,000 in connection with the kidnapping and sentenced to 15 years in prison. He had obtained the money by convincing the editor of the *Washington Post* that he would recover the baby from the kidnappers. Colonel Lindbergh was called to give evidence in the case of Curtis, who had told him that Betty Gow was involved in the kidnapping. Curtis was found guilty by the jury on 3rd July 1932, and received a prison sentence of 12 months and a fine of $1,000 (£200). It had transpired that John Curtis hadn't just given false reports but, in order to safeguard his own personal security, had deliberately prevented the kidnappers from being arrested.

In August 1932, secrecy surrounded the birth of the Lindbergh's second son, but in February 1933 the family were once again back in the newspapers concerning reports that two men had been arrested in connection with another kidnap threat to a Lindbergh child. The Colonel paid a cheque for £10,000, which one of the perpetrators tried to cash and the men were arrested. Four months later, police were on the trail of a man named Charley Maccord, alias Stanley, who was believed to be in possession of a large part of the ransom paid for Charles Augustus Lindbergh, the couple's firstborn son. Another man, Stewart Donnelly, using the name Eaton and believed to be part of Al Capone's gang, was being held by the French authorities in Paris. The two men were known to be linked, but this is where the trail went cold.

In September 1934, two and a half years after the kidnapping of Charles Lindbergh Jr, a 35-year-old German named Bernard (Bruno) Richard Hauptmann, used banknotes from the ransom in a petrol station and was arrested. He was then identified by a Dr Jafsie Condon as the kidnapper who had received the ransom in the New York cemetery, as well as being identified by a taxi driver who had been asked by Hauptmann to deliver a note to Dr Condon. Hauptmann was found to be in possession of a large part of the ransom money (£2,700) and was charged with extortion by a court in the Bronx. Another suspect, Henry Uhlig, was also questioned for several hours, but later released. Hauptmann maintained his innocence throughout and pleaded not guilty. When most of the ransom money was discovered at Hauptmann's address, he was indicted for the murder of the Lindbergh baby, and Colonel Lindbergh was one of the first witnesses to give evidence. Handwriting expert Albert Osborne identified the accused's handwriting on the ransom notes, which was confirmed by the way in which Hauptmann wrote the letter "x" (the German had a particular style of forming the letter by joining the two letters "es". Betty Gow was also called to the stand as a witness in the trial, and told the court how she had seen Hauptmann close to the Lindbergh's home in early March 1932. The trial eventually began on 2nd January 1935 in the small courthouse at Flemington, New Jersey. When Anne Morrow Lindbergh was called as a witness, she stood erect and spoke slowly and clearly. She was visibly emotional when she talked of playing with her baby son on the afternoon prior to his kidnap.

Mrs Lindbergh had spent a great deal of time with her son on that fateful day, including helping to get him ready for bed. She was asked to identify the clothes the child had worn on his last day at home and her eyes filled with tears.

It appeared that Hauptmann's fate hung on his handwriting. It was also suggested that he was a chiseller, and not the actual kidnapper, but the crucial link in the chain of evidence was the establishment beyond all reasonable doubt that Hauptmann was the writer of all the ransom letters, particularly the earlier ones. Hauptmann's fingerprints were never found on the ladder that was used to climb into the nursery and remove the child from his cot. Next came a dramatic twist when a new witness for the defence, Walter Manley, a painter contractor, confirmed the story of the accused's wife that Hauptmann had been drinking coffee at 7.15pm in a Bronx restaurant at the time the baby was kidnapped. There was also further speculation surrounding the actions of Violet Sharpe, while Hindegard Alickander, a new witness, testified that she had seen Hauptmann following Jafsie Condon on at least two occasions. According to newspaper reports, Hauptmann was offered protection if he agreed to reveal the identity of his accomplices. However, in the witness box Hauptmann declared how he had been at home on the night that the ransom money was paid (and not in the New York cemetery), playing his mandolin at a music party. On 25th January 1935 he stated: "Alive or dead, I never saw the Lindbergh baby." He told the jury how the ransom money had been given to him for safekeeping by a German friend, Isador Fisch. She later died of tuberculosis and Hauptmann discovered that he had been left with a great deal of money and he spent some of it. During a tense day of questioning by Attorney General Wilentz, he was quizzed on his badly written English and the way in which the ransom notes matched with Hauptmann's spelling of certain words, including "Wrihgt" for "Wright", and "boad" for "boat".

After 11 hours of deliberating, the jury found the German carpenter guilty of the kidnap and murder of baby Lindbergh. The jury of eight men and four women reached their verdict at 1am on 14th February 1935. After being sentenced to death, the condemned man spoke to two reporters saying: "I haven't a dollar and must depend on public help for my appeal. I am absolutely innocent, otherwise I would have said so at the beginning. I had five witnesses to show I was in the Bronx at that time, and they should have been believed. My greatest regret at being sentenced is on account of my wife and child." Asked if he was afraid of death, Hauptmann said: "No. I guess you'd feel the same as I do if your conscience was clear and your heart clean." His appeal began in June 1935 and was in stark contrast to the trial at Flemington, with a battery of arc-lights and hundreds of spectators. For the first time in history, wireless broadcasts with condemning comments about the prisoner, overheard by the jury, were cited by the defence lawyers as an influence altering the true course of justice. The appeal failed and a further appeal was represented to the United States Supreme Court in late 1935. Meanwhile, the definite impression that Hauptmann wasn't the murderer was gaining ground fast within the authorities and the press. The Supreme Court refused to review the case.

In December 1935, the Lindberghs and their 3-year-old child, Jon, set sail for Liverpool, amidst fears that the boy had been threatened with kidnap. It was also cited that the family wished to be far away from the US when Hauptmann was executed in January 1936. However, the German was granted a respite of 30 days by Governor Hoffmann of New Jersey on 16th January, who was not entirely satisfied with the case.

While Hauptmann remained in jail, a new suspect, disbarred lawyer Paul Wendel, admitted that he had written his signed confession after being tortured. According to a representative of the Brooklyn District Attorney, Wendel claimed he had been imprisoned for 10 days before signing the confession and that during this time he was tortured with fire, strung up by his thumbs to the ceiling and threatened with being placed in a "death-barrel" of cement lowered into the ocean if he didn't confess. He also said that four men burned his eyebrows and body with cigarettes. This was all reported in the newspapers on the same day – 3rd April 1936 – that Hauptmann was to face death by the electric chair. The condemned man was eventually executed for the murder of baby Lindbergh in May that year, but his widow continued the fight to clear her dead husband's name. When the Lindberghs returned to the US in December 1937, they were bombarded with telegrams from an organization called the Citizens' Protection League asserting, despite proof, that Hauptmann was not the baby's killer. The first telegram signed by the association's chairman, Kurt Mertig, read:

"Respectfully express opinion Hauptmann wasn't guilty of the kidnapping and murder... Mrs. Hauptmann is bereft of support, in dire distress. Please do something if you can."

Mary McElroy

(1933)

Twenty-five-year-old Mary McElroy, was kidnapped in June 1933 while she was taking a bath. On 3rd June, seven men said to have been concerned in kidnapping Mary, the daughter of the Kansas City Manager (the equivalent to a lord mayor), were arrested. At the time of their arrest, the kidnappers said that Mary was a "good person to abduct", and that they "would recommend her to other kidnappers". The young woman was even presented with a bunch of flowers by the leader of the kidnapping gang, and the victim herself was cited as saying to reporters that her "adventures had been good fun".

However, what appears to have been the "courteous" side of kidnap, when considering other darker, more dangerous and less dignified cases, came to an abrupt end on 28th July 1933 when Walter McGee was sentenced to death for the part he played in abducting the daughter of a judge. Mary had been taking a bath when two gunmen appeared and ordered her to dress and go with them. She was released the following day on payment of £6,000 by her father. The police stated that McGee made a full confession. While in the custody of her kidnappers, Mary was chained in a cellar at a bungalow and given crime novels to read. Obeying her kidnappers' instructions, Judge McElroy handed the ransom money to masked men outside the city, and later his daughter was returned. When Mary was released, and McGee was apprehended by police, he stated: "We did not intend to harm the young woman. We just wanted an easy pay off." He named his brother George as a collaborator, together with Clarence Click and Clarence Stevens. Click was then also arrested.

Despite Mary's claim that she had had fun on her short imprisonment, she collapsed outside the house where she had been held. McGee appealed against the sentence, which was due to take place on 2nd October 1933. Nicknamed the "courteous kidnapper", McGee was spared his life for his chivalry in presenting Mary with a gift of red roses. He should have been the first man to die under the United States' new "anti-kidnap law", however, due to his actions, his sentence was commuted to life imprisonment. It had been Mary's pleas that had helped to save him. Mary had been unharmed during the kidnap and felt strongly that death was too harsh for her kidnapper. There were rumours on both sides of the Atlantic that she had secretly fallen in love with the man who had broken into her family home and forced her from her bath, but this was vehemently denied by the victim.

Judge H F McElroy had also helped in the fight for the kidnapper's life and McGee – having had his death sentence suspended for three weeks – was finally told on 27th May 1935 that his life was spared. The former condemned man became hysterical on hearing the news, yelling with delight and hugging his warders and the prison bars. Mary McElroy, during a transatlantic phone call with a special representative writing for the *Daily Mirror*, said that she was "very happy" about the decision. With a sob in her voice she asked: "Why are people so cruel? I am not in love with McGee. I have never been in love with him, but when he kidnapped me he treated me with courtesy and chivalry." Asked if she would visit the prison to see McGee, Mary McElroy said: "Perhaps I shall... but not yet for a while." During the call, Mary shared the fact that by her side, at her home, was one deep red rose – all that remained of the bouquet that her courteous kidnapper had sent her.

Five years later, Mary McElroy was back in the newspapers when it was announced that she had shot herself dead in her Kansas City home on 21st January 1940. A friend told the press that she had been grieving for her father who had died the previous summer. Mary, who was just 32 years old at the time of her death, was found on the living room floor. A bullet wound was found in her forehead.

Brooke Hart

(1933)

On 17th November 1933, a newspaper report in San Jose, California, announced that the son of a wealthy merchant of the town, Brooke Hart Jr, had been killed by the gang that had recently kidnapped him. Two suspects were arrested and a local lawyer, Losis O'Neal, stated that one of the suspects had confessed that Brooke Hart was killed shortly after his kidnapping. The paper also reported that, according to the kidnapper, Brooke's body had been thrown into San Francisco Bay.

Shortly after Brooke had disappeared, a telephone call was made to his father's house, informing him that £8,000 must be paid, along with the words: "... if you want to see your son alive". The alleged confession stated that Brooke Hart Jr had been "beaten to death" before this phone call was ever made. In actual fact, the victim hadn't died as a result of a beating.

Less than 10 days later, the two suspects in the case were dragged out of the San Jose prison by a mob of angry locals and rushed to St James's Park with ropes around their necks. In an effort to keep back the crowds, the police hurled tear-gas bombs. However, a mad rush was made and the police were powerless to protect the two men. Several people were injured in the ensuing chaos. The mob then discovered that one of the men they'd pulled from the jail was the wrong man and they returned to the prison to secure the right man. Once both suspects were identified, the mob dragged the men about 100 yards before hanging them. One of the men, Thomas Harold Thurmond, was actually unconscious when he was hanged, but the other man, named as Jack Holmes, revived and showed resistance after throwing the rope from his neck. The mob forced the rope back on and Holmes was lifted, kicking, into the air. Thousands of onlookers cheered this horrendous spectacle, while the sheriff was also beaten unconscious and had to be taken to hospital. Sheriff William Emig had pleaded with Governor Rolph to place the two men in custody under protection from the National Guard when news of the lynching was announced, but the Californian governor had refused.

When the angry mob broke down the door of the jail, a vast crowd had started to gather, drawn by the shouting of the main perpetrators. The lynching was the outcome of vigorous agitation for the enforcement of the new law to make kidnapping a capital offence. On 28th November 1933 the governor of California, James Rolph, responsible for law and justice in the state, announced that anyone arrested in connection with the lynching and murder of the two suspects would be pardoned.

Brooke Hart Jr's body was eventually discovered on the mud flats of San Francisco Bay, which corroborated the story of one of the two arrested men. It was this that had sparked the fury within the town of San Jose and led to the mob dragging the men from jail. According to the *Central News* report of the lynching, the mob was led by a student – a friend of Brooke Hart Jr – from Santa Clara

University. Women were reported to have egged the men on, and when Thurmond was brought out of the jail, he was beaten by the women before he was hanged. It was alleged that after the hanging, Thurmond's body was cut down, petrol was poured over it, and it was set alight while women danced around the flames. Holmes's body didn't suffer the same fate, but only because there was no more petrol available. Newspaper photographers had their cameras broken so that no pictures of the lynching could be released, while after the men were dead, the mob broke branches from the city park's trees as souvenirs. However, a few photographs did make it into the north Californian press, but the faces of those in the mob were smudged to make identifying them nigh on impossible.

The lynching of the two suspects had been inevitable. Brooke Hart had worked at Hart and Son department store for his father, Alickander Hart, for much of his youth and was well-known and liked within the local community. When his body was discovered on 26th November 1933, washed up on the mud flats of the bay, the news soon spread and it wasn't long before radio reports mentioned that the lynching would be held on Sunday at 9pm. After graduating from university, Brooke Hart had been made vice president by his father with the intention that he would take over the family business when Alickander retired. The fact that the young man had been killed in such a frenzied and merciless way, even before the ransom demand was made, led to a public outcry. The people of San Jose and northern California wanted justice, and they wanted it fast

Twenty-two-year-old Brooke Hart was kidnapped on 9th

November 1933 when he left the family department store to collect his roadster from a downtown garage. He was picked up by five captors, driven to San Mateo-Hayward Bridge (while one followed in Hart's own car) and hit over the head with a concrete block. This didn't kill him, and neither did the fact that his kidnappers then threw him off the bridge. He landed in just a few feet of water at the base of the bridge while the tide was out. It was for this reason that his kidnappers then decided to shoot him. The bullets dealt the fatal blow that sealed the young man's fate.

A few hours later, the Hart family received the telephone call demanding the £8,000 ($40,000) ransom. Brooke Hart's car was found abandoned in Milpitas, seven miles east of San Jose. After two phone calls on Thursday 9th November, the night Hart was kidnapped and murdered, the family heard nothing until the following Monday, when a card posted in Sacramento arrived at the department store. A second card with the same postmark arrived on the following day. Alickander Hart had been instructed, on the Monday, to be ready to drive – with the ransom money – to the drop-off point when instructed. Mr Hart, however, had never learned to drive. Despite the fact that the Hart family placed a card in the window of the department store stating that Alickander Hart could not drive, other cards arrived requesting that he drive with the ransom money once instructions were sent.

The police picked up Thurmond, who was found acting suspiciously in a phone box, on the evening of 15th November, at about the same time that the Hart family received another anonymous phone call. He was arrested on suspicion of the crime and after hours of questioning gave the name Jack Holmes as his accomplice, before signing a confession.

Governor Rolph was publicly condemned by former US President, Hoover, for his inaction to protect the two men in custody and his blatant support of the lynching. Holmes' family tried to sue the governor, but Rolph died in 1934 and the suit was dropped. President Roosevelt also condemned the lynching, but while seven suspects were arrested, none were ever convicted. The actions of Thurmond and Holmes brought about the first lynching that actively involved politicians, business leaders, civic leaders and the media. While the actions of the two suspects, who had not been tried and convicted of the crime, should have been followed up and the two men brought to court, the lynching was a truly horrific example of society – with the knowledge and support of the authorities – taking matters into its own hands. Perhaps it would have been more prudent for the other members of the kidnapping gang to have been tracked down and arrested for their part in the tragic death of Brooke Hart, and the full story untangled, before mob rule (which acted as judge, jury and executioner) reigned swift and cruel justice on the two men. There were no winners here, just a town left devastated by the death of one of its promising young businessmen and a sorry excuse for justice.

June Robles and William Gettle
(1934)

Within a few hours of each other, two victims of the kidnapping wave, which terrorized the Western States of America, were found in May 1934. June Robles, the 6-year-old granddaughter of a wealthy cattle baron of Tucson, Arizona, was chained in an iron cage hidden in the cactus covering an abandoned quarry in the desert, nine miles from her home. She had been held prisoner as a kidnap victim for 20 days.

Meanwhile, William Gettle, a multimillionaire magnate, was discovered when police raided a house at La Crescenta, near Los Angeles. He had a mask over his face and his hands were bound with adhesive tape. In neither case had the big ransom demanded been paid. Three men and two women were arrested for the kidnapping of William Gettle. Extra police had to be hurried to the Los Angeles jail as soon as it became generally known that some of the kidnappers had been arrested and brought there.

Hundreds of men and women, infuriated by the series of kidnapping outrages in all parts of the United States, and especially by the treatment of June Robles, surged outside the jail calling for summary justice for the gang. The five prisoners were surrounded by a guard of heavily armed police, ready to frustrate the mob should the jail have been stormed. According to the *Central News*, the authorities declared that they would ask for the death penalty for the men, under the new California "Lindbergh" law that was passed after the outcry following the kidnapping and murder of Colonel Lindbergh's son. June Robles had suffered no injuries, but it was apparent that the memory of her terrible ordeal would remain with her for the rest of her life.

June had been found following the receipt of a letter by her uncle, who passed it on to the police. It was evidently from one of the kidnappers and indicated where she could be found. A posse of State Police immediately went to the spot and released her. June was rescued covered in dirt and in a pitiable state. An adequate supply of food (including biscuits, bread, potato chips and crackers) and water was within her reach, but it was evident that she had been too terrified to eat much. She had lost weight and was very hungry and weak. The little girl showed that she was making good progress following her release. It appeared that the kidnappers, or one of them at least, was afraid the child might die, and sent a letter to let her family know where she was. William Gettle, for whom a ransom of £15,000 had been demanded, was released after five days in the hands of his captors, following a spectacular raid by police and sheriffs on a small house at La Crescenta. He was unharmed, although he was worn out and haggard after his ordeal. William Gettle was discovered as the result of the arrest of a man and two women who were traced through a phone call made to the victim's family by a man from a chemist's shop, during which the name of the house in La Crescenta was named.

On 17th May 1934, the kidnappers' fate was reported in the *Daily Mirror*, it read: "Justice has never been meted out so promptly, say the *Central News* from Los Angeles, as it was last night on the three terrified kidnappers, Larry Carrigan, James Kirk and Royal Williams, concerned in the kidnapping of Mr. William F. Gettle, the oil millionaire." There was a general belief that the three men would be lynched and, as the prisoners became more and more terrified at the prospect, they agreed to plead guilty. The trial was staged in record time, with the judge passing sentence of life imprisonment in each case.

"Meanwhile, at Tucson (Arizona)", the *Daily Mirror* report continued, "the police are piecing together all available clues that may put them on the trail of the kidnappers who abducted six-year-old June Robles, three weeks ago, and then left her, a prey to a scorching sun and starvation, in a hole in the desert." At this time, it was also revealed that in the week June was eventually found, her father, Fernando Robles, on four occasions drove close by and within sight of the cactus heap under which the little girl's living tomb was hidden. This hole, where June described being left with the ants, was examined by County Attorney Houston and Chief of Police Wollard following her rescue, but it wasn't until much later in 1934 that her kidnapper was caught.

Agents of the Federal Department of Justice, after a six-month search, arrested Oscar H Robson on a charge of kidnapping June Robles while the child was on her way out of school at the end of the day. In newspaper reports, the department stated that a federal complaint was being filed charging Robson with sending extortion letters through the United States mail. The 31-year-old, a resident of Tucson, was alleged to have been identified by various handwriting experts, who declared that the handwriting of the extortion letters demanding £3,000 was that of Robson. However, after being formally charged with kidnapping, Robson was released on £10,000 bail. June had been abducted in broad daylight by Robson as she left school and went to make her way to her aunt's house. Robson had told her that he was taking her to his own house where her father was waiting for her. The small child had no reason to doubt the man's story and willingly got into his sedan. When June was seized, on 25th April 1934, onlookers and other parents had assumed at the time that she was with someone she knew. All charges against Robson were eventually dropped, and while a man came forward with more information, no further arrests were made and no convictions were ever forthcoming.

The two women arrested in Gettle's case were eventually sent to a reformatory and the oil tycoon (reportedly worth about £3.5 million at the time of the kidnap) received further threatening letters in the days and weeks following his release. His disabled wife died just a year after his kidnapping, while Gettle himself died of chronic liver problems in 1941.

Robert Cosgrove Greenlease Jr

(1953)

"Motor millionaire Robert Greenlease, 71, sat by the telephone in his Kansas City home all yesterday waiting in vain for word of his son Bobby, six, kidnapped from his school" wrote the *Daily Mirror* on 30th September 1953. A red-haired, larger-built woman, aged about 35, had called at Notre Dame de Sion Roman Catholic School in Kansas City, and told the nun in charge that she was Robert Greenlease's aunt. She said that the boy's mother had been taken gravely ill and that the chauffeur would not be calling for Bobby, as was usual, but that she would take him home at once. The woman, who was weeping, spoke convincingly about the Greenlease family. The nun instructed for Bobby Greenlease to be brought to the woman and she drove away with him from the safety of his school.

By 5th October 1953, there was still no word as to where the boy was being held, or with whom. The City's banks were instructed to stay open all day and all night so that his father could draw money immediately should a ransom demand be made for his kidnapped son. Newspapers reported that the "distraught" kidnapper had been persuaded by nuns at the convent, where Bobby was a pupil, to stop at the chapel to pray for the boy's mother, who they believed was gravely ill. The woman then left the school with the child in tow in a taxi and was last seen changing into a private car. Since that time, there had been no word and no sightings of either Bobby Greenlease or his kidnapper. Over the first weekend that the boy was missing, a spokesman for the family said: "We hope our faith can endure forty-eight hours" – this being the legal time limit before the Federal Bureau of Investigation (FBI) could be called into the case on the presumption that the child had been taken across a state border. Meanwhile, thousands of lorry drivers were asked by their union to keep a lookout for the child. But, good news was to evade the Greenlease family and on 8th October 1953, writing from New York, Stan Mays said: "Six-year-old Bobby Greenlease was found dead in a shallow grave today, forty-eight hours after his millionaire father kept faith with his son's kidnappers and paid the £210,000 ransom."

Bobby Greenlease had been shot. There was a posy of daisies in his grave in the backyard of a house at St Joseph, Missouri. A man and a woman, who were arrested, denied killing the boy and implicated another man who was then sought by the FBI. Police believed that Bobby had been dead already when the ransom money was dropped over a bridge near his home in Kansas City over the weekend. His body was found after they arrested Bonnie Brown Heady, 41, and Carl Austin Hall, 37, in St Louis and recovered half the ransom money. Heady was said to have admitted taking Bobby away from his school 10 days earlier by posing as his aunt and saying his mother was ill. But she denied knowing she was part of a kidnap plot. Hall, the son of a Kansas City criminal lawyer, was said to have told the FBI that he had planned the kidnapping after spending £7,000 inheritance left to him by his father two years before.

Both Heady and Hall alleged that Hall had killed the boy, but in a later statement they both blamed ex-convict Thomas John Marsh, 37, who had twice been sent to prison for offences against young children. A nationwide hunt then ensued for the missing man and Marsh's photo was shown in news items across the country. The St Louis police said that some of the ransom money and a pistol with three discharged cartridges were found in Hall's room at the hotel where he was arrested. The police alleged that Hall told them that he and Marsh kept the boy in the basement-garage of Heady's house. Hall was also alleged to have said that he found the pistol beside the boy's body, the same pistol that he had given to Marsh two or three days earlier. "I don't know what I did after finding the body", Hall's alleged statement ran. But police said he later admitted wrapping the body in a plastic bag and burying it in Heady's backyard: "because I had to get rid of it". Meanwhile, Heady was said to have told police that she had been "half drunk since the kidnapping".

Bobby wasn't frightened when Heady took him from school, she told police. She continued: "He was such a sweet child. He came along so nice. He talked about getting a dog and ice cream." It was alleged at the time that Heady said she had handed the boy to Hall a few blocks from the school. It was also said that Hall had handwritten the ransom letters to Bobby's father, Robert Greenlease. The first letter arrived on the night Bobby was kidnapped. The address on the envelope had been written by Bobby. A second letter, containing Bobby's school class pin, had arrived on the Friday after he went missing, and instructed Greenlease to put the advertisement: "Will meet you in Chicago" in a newspaper, if he agreed to deliver the ransom money to the bridge. The advertisement was inserted and two family friends drove to the bridge with the money. Later, it was alleged, Hall telephoned Greenlease that he would send a telegram from Pittsburgh the next day, with the address where Bobby could be found. Then the police in St Louis received word that Hall, staying at a local hotel, was spending "big money". They investigated and found what they said was part of the ransom money.

Despite blaming Marsh for shooting the boy, on 13th October 1953 Hall signed a confession that he killed Bobby. The news was released to the world by Chief of America's G-Men, J Edgar Hoover. The federal government had, by now, taken over the case by filing kidnapping charges against Hall and Heady who were both arrested on charges of extortion. It was then discovered that the lime used within the shallow grave had been bought by Hall before the boy's abduction. Because Bobby had been taken across a state line, the involvement of the FBI was necessary under the Federal Lindbergh Law, which provided for the death penalty if a kidnap victim was harmed. Meanwhile, a bullet in the floor mat of the station wagon owned by Heady was identified as having been fired from Hall's gun, but he said he could not remember what had happened to the other half of the ransom money, which had yet to be recovered.

Then, on 25th October 1953, a third arrest was made. Elizabeth Eleanor Curti, 29, a resident of a St Louis hotel, was charged with "having knowingly furnished false and misleading information to FBI agents". On 19th November 1953, Bonnie Brown Heady was sentenced to death by a Missouri courtroom. It was reported that she would die "in a bathing costume". Having been sentenced in Jefferson City to go to the gas chamber on 18th December 1953, Warden Ralph Edison of the state prison said that: "Mrs Heady will die wearing a two-piece bathing costume", while Hall, sentenced to the same death: "would wear bathing trunks for death". He explained that prisoners being executed were dressed as lightly as possible because their clothing was hard to decontaminate of cyanide gas. On the day that both Heady and Hall faced the gas chamber, neither would say what had happened to the missing ransom money.

Described in the press as a "pudgy-faced" widow, Heady was allowed five minutes with her accomplice, Hall, prior to her execution on 18th December. When the two emerged from the cell, Hall had lipstick smudges on his mouth and chin. As Heady was led blindfolded to the gas chamber she told guards: "Thanks for everything. You've been very kind." As the couple were strapped into their chairs in the gas chamber they talked quickly together as guards watched through the plate-glass window. It is not known what was said between them as they prepared to die, for within seconds a prison warder pulled a lever that sent a white cloud of cyanide gas rising from the floor into the eight-sided chamber. Hall took a big gulp, collapsed and died almost instantly, but Heady, the first woman to die in the gas chamber, held her breath until the fumes enveloped her. Their joint execution came 81 days after they kidnapped Bobby.

Officials who spoke to both Heady and Hall just before their deaths said: "neither had expressed real sorrow for the crime".

Peter Weinberger

(1956)

"Drama of kidnap note" read the headline in the *Daily Mirror* on 6th July 1956 as a distraught mother and father, sick with worry, waited in their home for the kidnapper of their one-month-old son to collect £700 in ransom money. "BUT THE KIDNAPPER NEVER CAME", wrote Ralph Champion from New York. Baby Peter had been kidnapped on 4th July. Detectives hid in the garden of the house in Westbury, New York, although the kidnapper had warned: "Don't tell the police". The hidden detectives watched as wealthy chemist Morris Weinberger placed a brown envelope by a tree near his garage. This was done in accordance with the kidnapper's instructions, left in a note when the baby, Peter, was snatched from his pram on 5th July 1956 on the porch of the Weinbergers' sumptuous home.

The note read: "I hate to do this but I'm in great need. I'm scared stiff. You must put 2,000 dollars, in small bills by the garage before two o'clock tomorrow or I'll kill your baby. I should ask for more but I'm asking only for what I need." The note continued: "Don't notify the police. I'm serious about this." However, Morris Weinberger did tell the police and it was on their advice that he followed what the note demanded. The brown envelope contained a packet of blank paper shaped like currency with real bills on the outside. Police then checked on servants who had been within the Weinbergers' employ. The Westbury police commissioner said: "This looks like an amateur job, probably the work of a distraught woman." Meanwhile, frightened parents in Westbury kept their children indoors as the detectives and the Weinbergers watched and waited.

Beatrice Weinberger made an emotional appeal on television several days later, urging the kidnapper to come forward by contacting her through a local church. Speaking emotionally she said: "We don't want revenge – we want our baby", and clergymen in New York kept a round-the-clock watch from 8th July 1956 in case the kidnapper or kidnappers contacted them about the disappearance of baby Peter. Betty (as Beatrice was better known) Weinberger's voice was shaking as she said: "Please, please use a church or a clergyman to make contact with us... they will not tell the police." In her tearful appeal she also pleaded for the kidnapper to look after her baby. This all followed the no-show in the Weinbergers' garden and the brown envelope left for the kidnapper who never came. Two days later, a phone call was made to the Weinbergers' Long Island home from a man demanding much more than the $2,000.

Nearing the end of August the search for baby Peter came to an end when his body was found in a wood. The torment of not knowing had ended, but the harrowing ordeal of dealing with his death had just begun. He had been dumped just 20 hours after being kidnapped. A taxi driver confessed to the kidnapping and alleged that he needed the ransom money in order to keep up hire-purchase payments on a refrigerator. Angelo John LaMarca, a married man and father of two, had loan sharks threatening him, debts and unpaid bills, when he happened to see Betty Weinberger wrap her son in a blanket and leave him in his pram on the porch while she popped back inside the house for a few minutes. Taking the baby and hastily leaving a ransom note demanding money seemed like the answer to LaMarca's prayers. He'd been driving around the area unsure as to how he could meet the demands for money being made on him, until he saw Mrs Weinberger.

Morris and Beatrice Weinberger wept when told by the police that their baby son had been found under a honeysuckle bush eight miles from their home. Although the kidnapper had never come forward to collect any ransom money, the Weinbergers had refused to believe that their cherished son was dead. Stocky taxi driver Angelo John LaMarca allegedly told the police how he had returned to the Weinbergers' home after taking baby Peter, intending to return the couple's son and take the ransom. However, when he saw the area swarming with police he had panicked and had dumped the baby in a wood. He hadn't intended that the baby should die, but he hadn't notified anyone as to where the baby could be found and this was viewed as murder as far as the jury was concerned.

In December 1956, the father of two who had been desperate to repay the hire-purchase on his fridge, was led from court in New York after being found guilty of kidnapping and murdering month-old Peter Weinberger. He had eventually been caught when his handwriting on a probation file – he had previous convictions for bootlegging – was spotted and matched to the ransom notes sent to the Weinbergers. He was sentenced to die in the electric chair and was executed at Sing Sing Prison on 7th August 1958. The only reason that LaMarca had taken baby Peter was because he saw him in his pram all alone on the veranda of the house – the kidnapping became a "spur of the moment" decision. It was a decision that was to cost two lives, including that of a tiny baby, and the devastation of two families. The case was unusual at the time in that the Weinbergers were not amongst America's rich and famous. Yes, they had some money, but they were a middle-class family – the archetypal average American citizens – and the kidnap of their baby son struck fear into the hearts of middle-class Americans across the nation. Almost overnight, people began locking their doors, where previously they'd had nothing to fear, and US citizens began to lose their sense of security. The kidnapping of baby Peter also prompted a change in the FBI's processes. Whereas before the Weinberger case it had been policy to wait for seven days in the event of a kidnapping, new legislation signed by President Eisenhower reduced this crucial time to just 24 hours. New legislation passed in 1998 gives federal officers the right to become involved in a kidnapping investigation before the 24 hours is up when it involves the protection of children.

Graeme Thorne

(1960)

The 8-year-old son of a couple who won £80,000 in a lottery was kidnapped on 7th July 1960. The kidnapper told the boy's parents in a phone call: "If you want him back safely, you must hand over £20,000".

The boy, Graeme Thorne, left his home in Bondi, Sydney, Australia in the morning to meet a family friend who normally drove him to school, but he never made it to the meeting place. The friend immediately drove to Graeme's house and told the boy's mother. After then driving to the school to see if Graeme had already arrived, but finding that he hadn't, the police were informed. The kidnapper phoned the Thorne home just 70 minutes after the abduction and demanded money off a police officer posing as Bazil Thorne. A full-scale police hunt was mounted immediately and the New South Wales Premier, Robert Heffron, broadcast an appeal. He described the kidnapping as "appalling" and urged every citizen in the state to join in the hunt for the little boy. Graeme's father, salesman Basil Thorne, who had won the lottery the previous month, made an appeal on television to the kidnapper. He broke down as he pleaded, "For God's sake, send Graeme back in one piece", while Graeme's mother, Freda, sobbed, "To have Graeme home safely we will pay out the whole £80,000." But Graeme was never to return home again.

In October 1960, a dramatic hunt for Stephen Leslie Bradley, who was wanted for the kidnap and murder of Graeme, ended when the British liner *Himalaya* docked at Colombo in Sri Lanka (at the time still known as Ceylon). Police boarded the London-bound liner and arrested 34-year-old Bradley. A warrant had been issued by a Sydney court charging him with the murder of the kidnapped child. Three hours after his arrest, Hungarian-born Bradley carried a battered brown suitcase down the gangway and was taken to the harbour police station. His wife and three children were also aboard the liner, which had left Sydney on 26th September 1960. The hunted man's family were to continue on their journey and leave the ship at Marseilles. Bradley was later taken back to the liner by the Australian high commissioner in Ceylon, to talk with his family before the *Himalaya* sailed at midnight. On 11th October, Bradley appeared before Colombo's chief magistrate who was to consider an application by the Australian government for his extradition. Meanwhile, two senior detectives flew from Sydney to Colombo to interview Bradley.

After having demanded £20,000 from the Thorne family for the safe return of Graeme, the kidnapper made no attempt to collect the ransom money. Children found Graeme's body in a shallow grave in a wood 10 miles north of Sydney. The boy had been tightly bound, gagged and wrapped in a blanket.

Then, on 19th October 1960, a magistrate in Sydney said there was "a strong presumption" that Bradley had murdered the 8-year-old boy and issued a warrant for the man's extradition from Ceylon to face a charge of kidnapping and murder. Extradition proceedings were expected to begin within a few days of the magistrate's statement in court. Many in the court had wept as Graeme's mother had described her last moments with her son before he set off from the family home to get a lift to school. Freda told the court how she had knotted Graeme's tie, peeled an apple for him and prepared his lunch. She also told the court about a visit she'd had from Bradley, whom she identified in a photo, three weeks before the kidnapping. Bradley, she declared, said he was a private inquiry agent looking for a previous tenant of the flat in which the family lived.

On 29th March 1961, women cheered and clapped in a courtroom in Sydney when Bradley, who had been extradited, was found guilty of Graeme's kidnapping and murder. Cries of "feed him to the sharks" were heard from the court when Bradley was sentenced to life imprisonment. The kidnapper had told Graeme's family that he would feed the boy to the sharks if his ransom demands were not met. There was, and is, no death penalty for kidnap and murder in New South Wales and when the judge, Mr Justice Clancy, announced the sentence there were scuffles and more shouts from the back of the court. Officials held back women as Bradley was taken down to the cells.

The kidnap of Graeme for ransom was the first of its kind in Australian history. The children who "found" Graeme's body had known for some time about "the rug" that had appeared at the site where they played, but it had never occurred to them that it was significant. It wasn't until two of the children mentioned the rug in passing to their parents that Graeme's body was discovered. The discovery of the small child's body caused massive shock in Australia. An examination of the body showed that he had been alive when he was hit on the head. Examination also revealed that Graeme had been murdered within 24 hours of his kidnap and that his body had been dumped soon afterwards. He was still wearing his school uniform and the carefully knotted tie that his mother had tied for him before he left home on the morning he disappeared. The case was also a classic case with regard to the forensic investigation. Graeme was found on a vacant allotment, yet the rug in which his body was found showed two plant types not found there. Added to this was the fact that there were tiny fragments of pink mortar on the body. The combination of the two plant types together (which was rare), the pink mortar and a blue car spotted close to the scene where Graeme should have been collected by the family friend brought the police investigation to a house in Moore Street in the suburb of Clontarf, Sydney. This was the house that Bradley had rented for his family before boarding the liner bound for London. Bradley had put the car up for sale and police linked the blue 1955 Ford to Graeme's body. Bradley was undoubtedly the kidnapper and murderer of this innocent young schoolboy.

Frank Sinatra Jr

(1963)

Singer Frank Sinatra kept to his hotel room in the gambling city of Reno, Nevada, on 10th December 1963, hoping for a telephone call from the kidnappers of his 19-year-old son, Frank Junior. Sinatra flew to Reno from his home in Palm Springs, California, soon after he heard the news that two gunmen had forced his son into a car at Lake Tahoe, a mountain resort close to the city of Reno.

G-Men (an American slang name for government men), worked with hundreds of armed police in the hunt for the kidnappers, although they were faced with a complete mystery. At this point, there had been no ransom demand and no apparent motive for the kidnapping. Earlier that day, two men had been suspected – Joseph Sorce, aged 23, and Thomas Keating, 21. Both were on the run from a Californian prison and were also wanted for alleged armed robbery and kidnapping, but the men were later arrested – and then cleared by the FBI of any connection with the Sinatra kidnapping. Sinatra Jr was abducted from his hotel room while he was waiting to give a show at the exclusive Harrah's Club. He had been appearing at the club with the band originally formed by the late Tommy Dorsey – the man who put Frank Sinatra on the road to fame. At the time of the abduction, 24-year-old trumpet player Jo Foss had been in the room. Foss told police that there was a knock on the door and a man's voice said: "Room Service". Sinatra Jr had opened the door and two men, armed with revolvers, burst in. Foss said that they forced him to the floor and gagged him before tying Sinatra's hands together with tape and hustling him out with a gun to his back. The police maintained road blocks over a wide area while others searched the snow-covered passes in the surrounding mountains, which rose to 7,200 ft. The police believed that Sinatra Jr might have been taken to one of thousands of motel rooms or hundreds of mountain cabins that had been closed down for the winter. A spokesman said: "It will take days to search the lot." When Frank Sinatra Sr was first told of the kidnapping, he exclaimed: "My God! I can't believe it." Close friend and fellow film star Dean Martin said in Hollywood: "Frank loves that boy very much. He adores him." Elsewhere in Hollywood, the boy's mother and former wife of the crooner, Nancy, was attended by a doctor for shock after hearing the news.

On 11th December, Sinatra awaited one of the cruellest notes that life has to offer: the ransom note. As the *Daily Mirror* reported at the time: "Of all crimes, none is quite so wretched as the kidnapping of a child or loved one." It is a timed and calculated agony, and as the newspaper continued: "In its own way, [it is] more sinister than murder itself. Suddenly the TV thriller explodes into terrifying reality. It is nasty. It is inhuman. The blackest of blackmail. A burden", says the paper, "feared by all rich men". Given that at this time anyone under the age of 21 was still legally a child, the kidnap was rightly expressed as the kidnap of a minor, despite the fact that at 19, in usual circumstances, Frank Jr would have been able to look after himself. Age just didn't count. Writing in the *Daily Mirror*, Roy Blackman was unforgiving of the kidnappers in his 1963 article in which he wrote: "When a child's life is in peril age does not count. The young Sinatra is not the first victim to be 'snatched' and he won't be the last." There had been 20 major kidnappings in the past 63 years in the United States. It was almost entirely an American crime. The Lindbergh Law had been passed four years after the kidnap and murder of Charles Lindbergh in the United States, making kidnapping punishable by death. By 1963, Europe had suffered little from kidnappers as compared to the United States. At the time, the worst case in Europe had been that of 4-year-old Eric Peugeot in 1961, the son of French car millionaire Roland Peugeot. The ingredients were all too familiar, however: a young son, a wealthy father and unscrupulous criminals. For 56 hours, the small child had been held captive until his father paid over £40,000 to the kidnappers. The family had received a note which threatened to torture the little boy to death if there was any kind of slip-up. Thankfully, all went to plan and the boy was returned to his family. The French public prosecutor had asked that an example be made of the two men eventually caught and tried for the crime, previously unknown in modern France, and they were given 20 years imprisonment. The wait for Frank Sinatra, however, was still on.

On 12th December 1963, Sinatra's son was on his way home. The ransom had been demanded and Sinatra had paid £85,700 for the boy's safe return. He said to journalists: "I've made no deal to protect the kidnappers. They are on their own now." Frank Jr had been found walking on a Los Angeles boulevard by a patrolling private eye. He told the private eye, George Jones, how he'd had a rough two-and-a-half days and that he believed his kidnappers to be "a bunch of amateurs" from the way they operated. He also stated that: "They were more scared than I was. One of them chickened out before they made the pick-up of the ransom money." It transpired that Sinatra had been in phone negotiations with the kidnappers before driving to a secret place on the Wiltshire Boulevard in Los Angeles to leave the ransom money in dollar notes. His son was then released onto the street by his captors. Frank Jr had been smuggled past TV cameras and reporters in the boot of George Jones's car to the home of his mother, Nancy, who was supported by her ex-husband. Sinatra Sr stated that the return of their son was about the best birthday present he could have hoped for: he was 46 years old that same day. However, while the family were left to celebrate Frank Jr's safe return, speculation was already building about whether the kidnap had in fact been a stunt.

Just one day later, a spokesperson for the family denied that the kidnapping had been a publicity stunt. The reason for the denial came after US newspapers and TV commentators had been remarking on "discrepancies" in stories of the kidnapping. One columnist noted the "strange coincidence" of Frank Jr's disappearance just as his father's latest film was being made, which included a scene about a kidnapping of somebody famous. Frank Jr remained quiet about the circumstances, following a request from the FBI who were still busy searching for the gang who had taken the young man.

The case caused quite a sensation on 14th December 1963 when it was released to the press that the FBI had secretly filmed the kidnappers collecting the ransom and that Frank Sinatra recognized two of the gang in the film. It was reported that two FBI agents had followed the crooner to the drop-off point in a garage and waited with a specially equipped cine-camera for members of the gang to appear. Just two days later, three men were in custody accused of the crime. Salesman Barry Keenan, 23, son of a wealthy stockbroker, and Joseph Amsler, also 23, were said to have gone to school with Frank Jr's sister, Nancy – although it was reported that she did not remember them. The third man arrested was John Irvine, a 42-year-old painter from Los Angeles. It was rumoured that the department of America's Attorney General, Robert Kennedy, which would prosecute the three men, was not expected to demand the death penalty at the trial set for January 1964.

"He sways gently above me, his voice softly caressing the microphone… 'Too close for comfort' he sings, and as the song ends his eyes are closed. From where I sit at a table butting on to the stage I could reach out and touch his shoes. But I am no fool. For this is the most closely guarded singer in show business. This is Frank Sinatra Junior, back singing again with the Tommy Dorsey band – with a voice which cost his father $240,000 in ransom money after last month's kidnapping", wrote a *Daily Mirror* journalist in January 1964. The reporter, who isn't credited for the piece, continues: "here in the tiny lounge of Harrah's Casino it is warm.

A few yards away hundreds of hopefuls are pouring their silver into platoons of one-armed bandits. Others crowd round the partitioning lounge bar to hear The Kid, as Sinatra Jr. is affectionately known. He is not worried [by the milling crowd]... within a few yards there are always big Ed Pucci and Joe Saitta. Big Ed, an amiable, wavy-haired, solid wall of a man, looks as if he could stop a tank. He used to be a professional footballer."

Big Ed had been drafted in as The Kid's constant companion. Joe Saitta, a taller, elegant man, was administrator for the entourage. However, despite the fan base, the attention and the hype surrounding the young singer desperate to follow in his father's footsteps, on 12th February 1964 there was a sensational charge made by the defence lawyers in the case of kidnap that it had all been a hoax. They claimed that the 19-year-old singer's abduction from a motel room was staged "so Frankie Junior could make the girls swoon as his papa once did", and that his actions were suspect: "from start to finish". The lawyers defending the three men accused of the kidnapping began with George Forde, counsel for Joseph Amsler, who told the Federal Court jury in Los Angeles:

"There is a vacant seat here for a fourth defendant. He is a financier who financed this whole thing. He paid for the hotels in Phoenix, Arizona, he paid for the liquor that two of the defendants and Sinatra Jr shared. He financed the rise of young Sinatra from a 100-dollars-a-week band-singer to an international star."

Forde continued: "Why, young Sinatra even preceded The Beatles on the Ed Sullivan TV Show." While Charles Crouch, defending Barry Keenan said: "The actions of Frank Sinatra Jr are suspect of chicanery from start to finish." The three men faced life imprisonment if they were found guilty, but their defence lawyers were out to prove that Frank Sinatra Jr had helped stage the whole episode. Nevertheless, the three men were convicted by a Los Angeles court in March 1964, and their defence teams then intended filing appeals for new trials on the grounds of insufficient evidence. The Sinatra family were then awarded damages over libel by Independent Television News in December 1965 and the Justice in the High Court announced that the substantial money would be given to the Sunshine Homes for Blind Babies and Young People. There was never any evidence to suggest that the kidnapping of Frank Jr had been a publicity stunt, despite what the TV company proclaimed in a news report. What the kidnap actually entailed was a half-baked act by witless amateurs that was poorly executed. Sinatra, with all his connections and ties to the highest echelons in both government and organized crime, always had the upper hand despite paying the ransom. Frank Sinatra Jr went on to become a well-known singer-songwriter and conductor.

Muriel McKay

(1969)

Despite the fact that the early part of the 20th century saw kidnapping mainly restricted to the US, with the country's famous and wealthy families fearing for their loved ones – particularly their children – kidnapping as a crime was not to stay on the other side of the Atlantic for long. On 30th December 1969, at around midnight, Scotland Yard launched a massive kidnap hunt for 55-year-old Australian, Muriel McKay, wife of Alick McKay, a director of *News of the World*. Muriel McKay's jewellery was missing from the couple's home in Arthur Road, Wimbledon, London and a machete, some string and some adhesive tape were found on the floor in a room at the address.

Alick McKay had arrived home at 7.45pm to find his wife missing. The contents of Muriel's handbag were scattered on the stairs and there were signs of a forced entry. At this point there was no ransom note and there was no evidence to show whether the director's wife had been hurt. McKay also found the telephone off the hook and was in no doubt that his wife had been forcibly removed from their home. The 60-year-old former director of the International Publishing Corporation (IPC) stated to reporters that, "there are other signs that there was force used against my wife". The police believed that Muriel had been kidnapped.

Just 24 hours after the kidnapping, a letter postmarked at

6.45pm on 31st December was sent from north London by Muriel to her husband, leading police to believe that she was being held somewhere in the capital. The letter, written in the victim's handwriting, made no mention of a ransom so Alick McKay made an appeal on TV to the kidnappers through his son-in-law, David Dyer, which read: "Will you please inform me what I have to do to get my wife back. What do you want from me? I am willing to do anything within reason. Please give me your instructions and what guarantee I have that she will be safely returned. I have had so many cranks communicate with me that I must be sure I am dealing with the right person." At the arrival of the letter from Muriel, police and family members were in no doubt that the woman was being held against her will and that parts of the letter may have been dictated. Detective Chief Superintendent William Smith, leading the search for Muriel, said: "The letter appears to have been written under some kind of duress." By 2nd January 1970, the police had received more than 100 reports from people who thought they had seen Muriel McKay, but after thorough investigations all of them proved to be innocent mistakes. Meanwhile, a medium brought in by the family to help with the disappearance felt that Muriel had been taken for spite or malice rather than money and that she was being held somewhere on Seven Sisters Road, north London. The family, believing that "anything is worth trying", also contacted Gerard Croiset, the Dutch medium who had so accurately pinpointed the whereabouts of missing people prior to the kidnapping. (It came out in the press after the trial that Croiset had predicted a white farmhouse north of London as being the place where Muriel was held.)

By 8th January 1970, more than 20,000 police officers were combing the streets of London alongside bombed and derelict sites, open spaces and forest land in the search for Muriel, but each and every outfit drew a blank. The staff at small hotels and boarding houses across London's 800 square miles were shown photographs of Muriel McKay in the hope that they had seen the missing woman. At the time, it was the largest concentration of police manpower ever used in Britain in trying to trace a missing person. Then the anonymous phone calls began and the police were confident that Muriel was being held captive for ransom. However, they were also looking into whether the housewife had left home of her own accord. By 3rd February, Muriel had been missing for 36 days and no ransom had been demanded.

However, seven days later, the police investigation led to a 17th-century farmhouse in the Hertfordshire village of Stocking Pelham, where villagers were shown a rusty machete (cleaver) found at the home of the McKays on the day Muriel went missing. Rook's Farm (a white farmhouse) was believed to have been a base where the missing woman had been held – at least for a time. Fingerprinting and other tests were carried out and the police held out hope that Muriel was still alive. An inch-by-inch search of the 10-acre farm was carried out and digging operations were begun, particularly where patches of earth showed signs of having been disturbed. It was also revealed that a man with a distinctive accent constantly called the McKay house and had demanded ransom money on several occasions, and there had even been arrangements to collect it. The man wanted McKay's daughter, Diane Dyer, to hand over £250,000 to a man she would meet on a bus. The handover was to be carried out, however, by a police officer dressed as Mrs Dyer. Detective Sergeant Wally White, dressed as a woman, boarded a No 47 bus at 5.45am from Catford, southeast London, to Stamford Hill in north London. He waited for the signal – a car behind the bus flashing its headlights – when he was then expected to get off the bus, walk to the car and hand over the money. The promise was that Muriel would be set free. There were two other detectives on the bus. Detective Chris Foreman was dressed as a paraffin salesman while Detective Sergeant Roger Street was disguised as a train driver. The kidnapper did not keep the appointment. Another call asked for a dawn meeting on 2nd February to hand over the cash. Ian McKay was to take his father's blue Rolls Royce to a point opposite a petrol station on the A10 in Hertfordshire. Roger Street was to pose as Ian McKay, driven by another officer dressed as a uniformed chauffeur. The money was placed between two paper sunflowers opposite the garage, as arranged, but after a three-hour wait, detectives decided that the kidnapper wasn't going to show up.

Then, 44 days after Muriel went missing, two brothers were charged with murdering the director's wife, although no body had been found. They were also accused of demanding £1 million by menaces from Alick McKay. Arthur Hosein, 33, and his

21-year-old brother Nizamodeen, were charged with the offences following 72 hours of questioning by police. Both brothers lived at Rook's Farm in Stocking Pelham. It transpired that two weeks before the arrests Alick McKay had been informed by police that it was unlikely his wife was still alive. However, top detectives were puzzled as to why there were no clues as to Muriel McKay's whereabouts. The investigation had led them to an area in Essex known as Sleepy Hollow, but a search there had been "fruitless". Meanwhile, the two brothers accused of Mrs McKay's murder were remanded in custody for a week. Their solicitor, David Coote, said that both men would be pleading not guilty to all charges.

By 21st February 1970, army deserter Roy Roper was sentenced to three years in jail for demanding £2,000 for the return of Muriel. He sent a letter to Alick McKay claiming he knew the whereabouts of the newspaper man's wife. In court, however, Roper claimed he didn't know why he sent the letter and pleaded guilty to attempting to obtain money by criminal deception. In April 1970, the Hosein brothers were charged with six further offences, including blackmail and threats to murder. There was uproar in court two months later when, on 9th June, Arthur Hosein jumped to his feet and shouted across the court. He struggled furiously with five policemen who had to hold him back while trying to calm him. On that same day it was also revealed that 78 statements had been made during the police probe into the two brothers' lives and that 22 prosecution witnesses were likely to be called to the trial. The brothers were sent for trial at the Old Bailey on 17th June, following the six-day hearing at Wimbledon Magistrates' Court, which ruled that there was sufficient evidence to show a case to answer for the murder charge and six other counts.

Perhaps even more shocking was the news in September 1970 that Muriel McKay had been kidnapped and murdered by mistake. The kidnappers had actually intended to abduct Anna Murdoch, claimed Attorney General Sir Peter Rawlingson, QC, because her husband, Rupert, was chairman of the *News of the World* organization. Sir Peter told an Old Bailey jury that a mix-up had led to the kidnappers snatching Muriel McKay after they followed a *News of the World* Rolls Royce to what they thought was Rupert Murdoch's home. Unknown to them was the fact that Rupert and Anna Murdoch were out of the country and that Alick and Muriel McKay had daily use of the chairman's vehicle during this time. The QC continued: "it was obvious that when they took Mrs McKay away, they thought they were abducting Mrs Murdoch". It was alleged that the kidnappers said they were members of an American Mafia gang and 18 telephone calls were made demanding money with menaces after Muriel McKay disappeared. However, the Hosein brothers continued to plead not guilty to all seven charges against them.

The words of the first phone call demanding a ransom were read out in court: "Tell Mr McKay it is the M3, the Mafia. This is the Mafia Group 3. We are from America, Mafia M3. We have your wife." The caller continued: "You will need £1 million by Wednesday. We have your wife. You will need £1 million to get her back. You had better get it. You have friends – get it from them." It was alleged that the caller also said: "We tried to get Rupert Murdoch's wife. We could not get her, so we took yours instead... have £1 million by Wednesday night or we will kill her." The letter written to Alick McKay by his wife just 24 hours after she went missing was also read out in court. It said: "Alick darling, I am blindfolded and cold. Please do something and get me home. Please co-operate or I cannot keep going. I think of you all constantly, and have kept calm so far. What have I done to deserve this treatment?" Sir Peter claimed that fingerprints on the letter belonged to Arthur Hosein. The court also heard how constant ransom demands were made yet Alick McKay was denied any proof that his wife was still alive and well. He had been subjected to a constant barrage of threats, menaces and demands for money since the time of his wife's disappearance and the arrest of the two men. However, despite lack of proof during the latter weeks of Muriel's disappearance, two further letters sent at the end of January were read out in court. Both were written by Muriel and postmarked Wood Green, London. The first was to her husband and read: "I am deteriorating in health and spirit. Please co-operate. Excuse writing. I am blindfolded and cold." The letter added: "The earlier you get the money the quicker I may come home, or you may not see me again, darling." In the letter to her daughter, Muriel wrote: "Negotiate with the gang as quickly as possible. The gang is too large to fool." She also thanked her daughter for looking after her father. The letters were accompanied by a ransom note asking for £500,000, on which it was alleged that Arthur Hosein's palm impression had been found, while further letters on 26th January contained fragments of wool and leather that were purported to belong to the clothing of Muriel McKay. However, at this stage there was no suggestion, or evidence, that she was still alive. And, according to one handwriting expert, there was a "considerable probability" that two of the ransom notes were written by Arthur Hosein. It was evident that the handwriting had been disguised, but the expert was clear that it was still written by the same person, after comparing it with six examples of handwriting taken from Hosein. It was also brought up in court how Arthur Hosein's younger brother, Nizamodeen, was in constant fear of his older sibling. This was backed up by a nurse, Mohorak Mohammed, who had spent some of the previous Christmas at Rook's Farm with the brothers. She described how the younger brother, who she called Nizam, had been kind and gentle to her, but that he was on edge and in fear of Arthur.

Giving evidence towards the end of September, Arthur Hosein told how he had been "tortured mentally and physically" by police and pointed at Detective Chief Superintendent Wilfred Smith of whom he accused: "His attitude was to beat the hell out of me while under the influence of drink. He had a bottle of Scotch in front of him. He spat in my face and hit my belly." The accused man also claimed that he had been starved for two nights and had not slept for two nights either, stating in the witness box that he had been woken by police every 10 minutes. He also denied statements that the police said he had made. He also shocked

Kidnap

the court with his allegations against his brother of meeting twice – at least – at Rook's Farm in the early hours of the morning – one of the men who visited at that time was believed to be the former Labour MP and millionaire publisher Robert Maxwell. The court was stunned to hear how Maxwell and three other men had been talking to Nizam while Arthur was asleep upstairs. However, Arthur Hosein heard voices and came down to find the four men with his brother in the sitting room, drinking whisky. He claimed that on the night Muriel McKay went missing he had gone to bed with a bottle of Scotch and some ginger because he was feeling unwell with a temperature. His German-born wife, Elsa Hosein, was away in Germany with their children and he thought he'd get some rest. He said goodnight to his brother just before 7.30pm and, on the way up to bed, realized that his car was not there. It was not unusual for Nizam to have used the car and Arthur described this to the court from the witness box. However, Arthur Hosein was also prone to outbursts in court, and even accused the judge of being "partial", for which he was bustled down the dock steps to the cells. Throughout his evidence, Hosein continued to deny any knowledge of Muriel McKay's disappearance and accused the police of beating him while in custody. He also accused Wilfred Smith of ordering him to make mis-spellings when specimens of his handwriting were taken. Hosein said: "I would have done anything rather than be beaten again." Paper and envelopes said to bear his fingerprints, on which ransom notes were written, must have been taken from his farmhouse, he said. When Sir Peter referred to a letter addressed to the *News of the World* and the matching indentation on paper found at Rook's Farm, including an impression of the words "St Mary", the name of the McKay home, Hosein said: "I would not put anything past the police to acquire a conviction in this case." Defence witnesses including farmers, friends and neighbours of Arthur Hosein gave evidence that, since the date of Muriel McKay's disappearance, Husein had appeared normal and went about his usual business.

On 24th September 1970, the Old Bailey jury heard how on the night Muriel McKay was taken from her home, Nizam Hosein had been visiting a third brother, Adam, just 20 minutes away. Adam Hosein, the middle brother, told the court that Nizam had called on him at 11.30pm on 29th December. Although he hadn't been expecting his younger brother's visit, he was not surprised, he told the judge. He stated how Nizam seemed perfectly normal and left around midnight. Also in court that day was handwriting expert Dr Julius Grant – called by the defence – who stated that either brother could have written the ransom notes. However, he also told the jury how "they could have been written by anybody". It was also the day that Elsa Hosein ended her evidence. She stated that when the police had first called at her home, she had no idea it was in connection with the McKay case and believed that the police were inquiring about stolen jewellery. Events also began to hot up in court.

On 25th September 1970, Nizam Hosein told the court about his relationship with his older brother, of whom he claimed he was scared. "When I didn't do something he thought I should do, he would have a go at me." He told the court that three nights before Muriel McKay was kidnapped he went to the police to complain that Arthur had beaten him up. Tears glistened in his eyes and rolled down his cheeks as he told the Old Bailey: "I was terribly afraid of Arthur." His voice was barely audible as he gave evidence on the tenth day of the trial. He went on to explain how he was responsible for all work at Rook's Farm and how he received no help or support from his older brother. He also stated that he thought it was: "obvious that Arthur had had a part in the McKay affair". He told of his growing suspicions at the strange things his brother forced him to do. These included planting paper flowers in a lane and ordering him to pick up dumped suitcases – which police alleged were part of ransom arrangements. Nizam said that he had thought at one point that they might be helping a woman to elope. Then he wondered if they were involved with stolen property. It was only after they were at a police station for questioning that the truth hit him, he stated. "It was the paper flowers that made me really frightened", he said. He then repeated how Arthur would often beat him if he did not do what he was told. He told the court how on 19th December he had gone to a car taxation office – without question – and, as Arthur Hosein had demanded, made inquiries about a News of the World car. He said that his older brother had told him to use a false name and say that the vehicle had been involved in a minor accident. He also told how he was ordered to plant paper flowers by a roadside in Dane End (where the police left dummy ransom money) and to go back later and collect suitcases. By this time, he said, Arthur had got out of the car and had ordered Nizam to pick him up later, after collecting the suitcases. Nizam told the court that he had been extremely suspicious by this time, but when he'd asked what was going on, he was told that he didn't need to know and that he should just do as he was told.

"I was not prepared to pick up suitcases unless I knew what it was about. We had a punch-up in the car and I jumped out", he claimed. He said that five days later, on 6th February, he was once again ordered to pick up suitcases – this time from a garage. Nizam had driven to the garage but became spooked when a car horn sounded. He had stayed for a while, but because the cases were white and not black as Arthur had said they would be, he decided to leave them. He explained how the following day police had shown up at the farm and Arthur had ordered him to keep his mouth shut. He was taken to Kingston police station where, he told the court, if he'd told the police the truth, he could have cleared himself of 90 per cent of his troubles. However, at this time, he was still being held alongside Arthur and was terrified of what his brother would do, should he tell the truth. He had kept quiet, he told the hushed courtroom. He denied all allegations that he was involved with a Mafia gang that may have included Robert Maxwell, and said there was no truth in the story that Arthur Hosein was telling. He stated that Arthur had cut out photographs of Maxwell from the newspapers and asked Nizam to tell the police that this was a man he had met with on several occasions. However, four days

Kidnap

later, Nizam Hosein was forced to admit to the court how he had stabbed one of his own brothers in Trinidad (which had led to one of two court appearances in his homeland). Under cross-examination by Barry Hudson, QC, who was defending Arthur, Nizam admitted to the stabbing, while counsel suggested that he was more than capable of dealing with a situation involving the possibility of violence. Nizam claimed that the stabbing had been an accident after one of his older brothers had approached him from behind and collared him. He claimed that he had turned around and the knife had stuck him. The QC then proceeded to question Nizam about a further charge in Trinidad a year later when he was charged with assaulting and beating someone. Nizam told the court how he hadn't been convicted, but that he had had to report to a probation officer every fortnight for three years.

A day later in court, it was alleged that Muriel McKay's death warrant had been signed the moment she was taken away. Sir Peter Rawlingson, QC, making the suggestion, was giving his final speech for the prosecution when he told the jury of nine men and three women: "You may think Mrs McKay, trussed and gagged, was forced into the boot of the car and taken away. Was there ever any thought of ever releasing her? If she was to be released, would she not have been able to identify those taking her?" Sir Peter also spoke of the absence of Muriel's body. He told the jury that subject to anything that the judge Mr Justice Shaw might say, he wanted to put it that they might be satisfied that there were such circumstances as rendered a crime certain. Also summing up, Barry

Hudson, QC, for Arthur Hosein said that assuming Mrs McKay was dead, the jury had to ask three important questions: 1) If she was dead, how did she die? 2) When did she die? 3) Where did she die? "I say with great respect," said Hudson, "and looking in every nook and cranny of this case, these three questions have not even been indicated by mere inference. The questions cannot possibly be answered."

Hudson also stated that Nizam Hosein had invented his evidence in order to save himself. He told the court how the younger brother would say anything that might implicate Arthur Hosein. However, Douglas Draycott, QC, defending Nizam told the jury: "You must consider the two defendants separately on each count. Don't lump them together." On 3rd October 1970, Draycott claimed that the key to the case was Arthur Hosein's mentality in his final defence speech. He claimed that Arthur had "behaved with considerable unreality". This included the fact that he'd alleged to have seen his younger brother talking to a group of men in the middle of the night, whom he claimed included Robert Maxwell. Draycott continued: "The cunning of it is this. Arthur knew that Mr Maxwell had been one of the contenders for the purchase of the News of the World and had lost that struggle. Mr Murdoch, the present owner of the newspaper, was successful and that was common knowledge. It must have seemed to Arthur Hosein's unreal mind that a jury would accept that Mr Maxwell would be involved because Mrs Murdoch was the woman intended to be kidnapped." He went on to describe Arthur's story as a "crazy invention". He also stated that Nizam had merely been a chattel – someone who would do as he was told. The judge, Justice Shaw, in his own summing up, told the jurors not to consider the charge of murder against the Hosein brothers until they had considered the other charges, including the kidnapping. "Unless you come to the conclusion, if you do, that it has been proved that one or both defendants was a party to kidnapping, there is no basis at all for a charge of murder", he said. "The snatching of a woman from her home and family anywhere is a crime which must arouse deep detestation and abhorrence. When such a crime takes place in a quiet suburb of a great metropolis, such as ours, it becomes more outrageous and horrific", he continued. He warned the jury, however, not to let emotion cloud their judgement.

On 6th October 1970, Arthur Hosein was jailed for life for the murder of Muriel McKay and sentenced to 25 years in jail for her kidnap. Nizamodeen Hosein was given a life sentence for murder and 15 years for kidnapping. In passing sentence, Justice Sebag Shaw, said: "The kidnapping was cold-blooded and abominable… she was reduced to terror and despair." Nizam was recommended for leniency by the jury, while Arthur Hosein shouted at the judge once sentence was passed. Justice Shaw went on to praise the police for a brilliant job saying: "The community owes a debt of gratitude to you [Detective Chief Superintendent Smith] and your colleagues. It was brilliantly done. There is no other way to describe it, and it has enabled justice to be done in this court." The jury – out for four hours – had found both brothers guilty on seven charges each. The judge also said in his summing up: "She [Muriel

McKay] was snatched from the security and comfort of her home, and was, so long as she remained alive, reduced to terror and despair. This will shock and revolt all right-minded persons, and the punishment must be salutary so that law-abiding citizens may feel safe in their homes." Both brothers were also sentenced to 14 years – the maximum penalty – for blackmail. The judge told the brothers: "You put Mr McKay and his family on the rack for weeks and months in an attempt to extort money through your monstrous demands." Each brother also got 10 years for threats to murder. For their services, each juror was exempted by the judge for jury service for 10 years. The Hosein brothers were driven from the Old Bailey prison yard in separate vehicles. Arthur Hosein was taken to Wandsworth prison while Nizam was transported to Brixton.

Speaking after the sentencing, Alick McKay said: "They have got a life sentence. I, too, have a life sentence, wondering what has happened to my wife. Those people in the dock, I feel, could have said what happened to my dear wife. They haven't said and I shall never know." He told of his terror when he arrived home to find his wife missing and after frantically searching the house and telephoning the police, he saw her glasses lying on the floor by the downstairs telephone. He just knew she hadn't left of her own free will. After 40 years of knowing Muriel and 35 years of marriage, he just knew.

Two hundred mourners attended a memorial service for Muriel McKay on 8th October 1970 in St Mary's Church, Wimbledon. Elsa Hosein promptly began divorce proceedings against Arthur in

November 1970, once the shock of sentencing had sunk in. In court, Judge Moylan granted Mrs Hosein an order to prevent her husband disposing of the proceeds from the sale of Rook's Farm, which had been auctioned earlier that month. Eight months later, Elsa was granted a divorce from her husband and was free to start a new life abroad with the couple's children.

Two years later, Rook's Farm – the scene of much searching during the tragic kidnapping of Muriel McKay – was once again in the spotlight when a wedding guest attending a reception at the farmhouse was found stabbed to death. John Scott, 26, had been involved in an argument at the wedding reception and suffered several stab wounds to the chest. Also in 1972, Arthur Hosein – who continued to proclaim his innocence – was given permission by the Home Office to produce new evidence that he claimed would prove he wasn't guilty of the crimes committed against Muriel McKay.

In 1990, Nizam Hosein was released from prison for good behaviour on the recommendation of the Parole Board and endorsed by the then Home Secretary, David Waddington, although Arthur Hosein was sent to a top-security prison in Liverpool, where he was officially regarded as being mentally unstable.

There has been no such reprieve for Muriel McKay's family. No one, except her killers, knows what happened to Muriel, how or where she was killed, or where her body, if indeed it remained in one piece, now lies.

James Cross and Pierre Laporte

(1970)

One of Canada's biggest ever police hunts was launched on 5th October 1970 after a gang, armed with machine guns, kidnapped a British diplomat. The gang forced their way into the home of 49-year-old James Cross, in a fashionable suburb of Montreal, before entering his bedroom and ordering him to dress. While his wife, Barbara, screamed in terror, James Cross was led handcuffed to a waiting taxi. The taxi-driver, who was also held at gunpoint, drove off with the kidnapped diplomat. Police said that a French-Canadian terrorist organization, the Quebec Liberation Front, had claimed responsibility for the kidnapping. But, they also announced that they had found a ransom note from another of the groups seeking independence for Quebec, the League of Patriots.

This note demanded £213,000 in gold for the release of Mr Cross. It also called for the release of 12 jailed terrorists and a plane to fly them to Cuba. Setting a 48-hour deadline, the note said that the group "would not be responsible for what happens to Mr Cross" if the demands were not met. Irish-born James Cross had been senior British trade commissioner in Montreal since 1968. The kidnappers got into his house by telling a maid who opened the door that they had a present for Mr Cross, who had turned 49 the week before. One of them produced a gaily wrapped parcel. Then, drawing their guns, the men forced the maid back into the house. Canada's special anti-terrorist squad was called into action after the kidnapping and police were alerted throughout the country. In Ottawa, Premier Pierre Trudeau had urgent talks with his top officials. Guards were put on other diplomats who it was thought might also be targets for the kidnappers. The Quebec Liberation Front (FLQ) had been held responsible for a series of bombings in Quebec during the 1960s.

Fears grew for the safety of James Cross as the 48-hour ransom deadline began to run out. Ministers of the federal and Quebec province governments held urgent meetings to consider the demands of the kidnappers, but by 6th October 1970, the day after the kidnapping, there was no indication that they had made any decision. The four men who had kidnapped James warned the police not to hunt for the diplomat, while an appeal was made to the kidnappers to allow their captive access to a drug that he needed. A doctor stated that without the drug the diplomat would be in grave danger within a few days. Writing from Montreal, reporter John Smith explained in a newspaper article that the terrorists had extended the deadline for the second time on 8th October. Commandos of the FLQ gave James another 12 hours to live. In a communiqué extending the deadline, the commandos said that unless their demands were met, "we will no longer have any choice except to kill Mr Cross". In a letter delivered to Mrs Cross two days after the kidnapping, James Cross wrote: "I am being well treated, but the FLQ are determined to achieve their demands." The kidnappers also repeated a rejection to the government's offer to negotiate for the release of James. One day later, the Canadian authorities then made a dramatic appeal for proof that the envoy was still alive. They wanted the terrorists who had seized James to get him to write to his wife saying: "It is now five days since I left. I want you to know darling, that I miss you every minute." By checking the handwriting, the authorities hoped to establish that he was safe before starting any talks with the kidnappers. Five suspects were already being hunted in a desperate race to save James Cross's life after the extended deadline passed without any word on 9th October. By 12th October, with still no word on the safety of the British envoy, the kidnappers had a second victim, Quebec Labour Minister Pierre Laporte. The 49-year-old was also threatened with execution by the gang if their demands were not met, but at this stage no one knew whether the first victim, James Cross, was alive or dead. In a tense war of nerves with the Canadian government, the terrorists repeated their demands. The Canadian authorities held crisis meetings and one source said that there was "a controlled state of panic" over the threat to Mr Laporte. Heavily armed guards were deployed to protect well-known politicians and public figures, while Quebec's City Hall looked like an armed fortress. Thousands of police joined Canada's biggest ever manhunt for the terrorists. The FLQ's "execution" threat came in two separate messages. Clipped to one note was Laporte's official parliamentary pass. A note apparently written by Pierre Laporte was found in a Montreal telephone box. The Minister told his wife and two children that he was safe and well but added: "The important

Marion Parker Marion Parker, the 12-year-old Los Angeles girl who was kidnapped in December 1927. She was later found dead despite her father having paid a ransom of £300. William Hickman, a 17-year-old bank clerk, was charged with her kidnap and murder.

Charles Lindbergh Jr Pioneering aviator Charles Lindbergh had captured the world's attention when he made the first solo non-stop crossing of the North Atlantic in May 1927. In *Spirit of St Louis*, a Ryan NYP single-engine monoplane, Lindbergh flew from Long Island, New York to Paris (Le Bourget) in 33 hours and 39 minutes. He covered a distance of 3,590 miles to win a prize of $25,000.

The front page of the *Daily Mirror* from 3rd March 1932 dramatically announces that Colonel Charles Lindbergh and his fellow airmen were aiding in the search for his kidnapped son.

The story was still front-page news more than a week later as an explanation was published of how the kidnappers managed to abduct one of the most famous babies in America.

The headline that the whole world had been hoping it would never see. Charles Augustus Lindbergh, aged just 20 months, had been found dead despite assurances that he would be returned unharmed.

Mary McElroy Mary McElroy with her father and brother after she had been released by her kidnappers. She declared that her adventure had been good fun, although Walter McGee was sentenced to death for the crime.

June Robles/William Gettle For once, a kidnap provided a happy ending when June Robles, the 6-year-old granddaughter of a wealthy cattle baron, was returned to her family following her ordeal. County Attorney Houston (bareheaded) and Chief of Police Wollard are pictured examining the hole in which June was chained for days by kidnappers in a desert-like region of Arizona. The hole was covered with cactus to prevent accidental discovery.

Frank Sinatra Jr
Sinatra Sr was one of the most prominent singers and actors at the time, so was an obvious target for kidnappers. During one ransom conversation in a telephone booth with his son's kidnappers, Frank ran out of money and was disconnected. This started his obsession with always carrying a roll of coins with him – just in case – that lasted the rest of his life.

Frank Sinatra Jr was abducted from the dressing room of the club where he was due to perform in December 1963. It was temporarily mooted by some that the kidnapping was a publicity stunt aimed at boosting the youngster's career.

This is Mrs Muriel McKay

HAVE YOU SEEN HER?

Daily Mirror Friday, January 2, 1970

out goes that £50 limit on travel

BOOM AHEAD FOR HOLIDAYS IN THE SUN

Muriel McKay The front page of the *Daily Mirror* asks the question that is on everybody's lips: have you seen her? Muriel McKay, the wife of a prominent *News of the World* director, had been kidnapped from her home.

DAILY Mirror

The McKay trial

Jury is told of woman's ordeal after a blunder by kidnappers..

'THEY TOOK THE WRONG WIFE'

QC's story of a £1,000,000 ransom plot

MRS. MURIEL McKAY was murdered by kidnappers who

NO MORE TALKS, SAY ARABS

The *Daily Mirror* breaks the news that the kidnappers abducted the wrong victim. The kidnappers' intention had been to kidnap the wife of the media tycoon Rupert Murdoch but a case of mistaken identity had led to his deputy's wife being taken instead.

Police organize a search of farmland near the home of Muriel McKay in their hunt for clues.

Despite the fact that Muriel McKay's body has never been found, brothers Nizam and Arthur Hosein were found guilty of her kidnap and murder and were jailed for their crimes. The brothers received life sentences for the murder plus a total of 40 years between them for kidnapping and blackmail.

The team of detectives who investigated the kidnapping and murder of Muriel McKay. When Alick McKay arrived home he found the contents of his wife's handbag strewn over the stairs and the telephone ripped from the wall. What followed next was a series of blunders by the police, bettered only by the mistakes made by the criminals themselves.

A police van containing the two Hosein brothers leaves court during the Muriel McKay murder trial.

DAILY MIRROR

Patty Hearst branded as 'armed and dangerous'

THE FUGITIVE

MISSING heiress Patricia Hearst has been branded "an armed and dangerous kidnapper" by the F.B.I. And they have issued a warrant for her arrest.

Patty, the all-American girl pictured above, is on the run with two "soldiers" of the terrorist group who call themselves the Symbionese Liberation Army.

They are William Harris, 29, and his wife Emily, 27, who face charges with Patty of kidnapping and armed robbery.

The new twist in the story of 20-year-old Patty, who was kidnapped more than three months ago, came in an announce-

From GORDON GREGOR in Los Angeles

ment from the F.B.I. in Los Angeles.

They say that Patty and the Harris couple went to Mel's Sporting Store in Inglewood, Los Angeles.

Mrs. Harris was buying clothing worth about £15 when shop assistants saw her husband putting a pair of 50p socks up his jacket sleeve.

He was challenged, guns were drawn, and the F.B.I. said that Patty, who was sitting in a stolen car, opened fire with an automatic rifle.

The trio got away in a stolen van, taking the driver, 18-year-old Tom Matthews as a hostage.

Robbery

He was held for twelve hours as they drove around. He said all three told him they were members of the S.L.A. and Patty said she had been in the San Francisco bank robbery.

She was referred to as "Tania" and she had a loaded automatic weapon.

Later a spokesman for the Hearst family said that Randolph Hearst, Patty's millionaire father, was "upset at...

Patty the terrorist—in a picture released by the "army" last month.

Patty Hearst The headline says it all... from kidnap victim to wanted fugitive in one fell swoop! Having been kidnapped and the subject of a ransom demand, heiress Patty Hearst switched sides and joined forces with her abductors in May 1974, a terrorist group calling themselves the Symbionese Liberation Army.

Lesley Whittle Lesley Whittle – pictured at her brother's wedding in 1972 – was kidnapped from her home in January 1975 and a ransom of £50,000 was demanded from her distraught mother.

A sketch artist's impression of the man wanted for questioning over the kidnap of heiress Lesley Whittle in January 1975. He was nicknamed the Black Panther and labelled the "most dangerous criminal at large in Britain" at that time.

Evidence in the crime case of the 17-year-old heiress. The picture shows the line-up of clues that police found in the kidnapper's abandoned car. There were punch tapes with ransom payment instructions, a cassette recorder – probably to carry a message from Lesley – and barley sugar and Lucozade (to feed her).

Lesley was found dead at the bottom of a drain shaft. Her coffin is carried from the tent-screened drain shaft to a waiting van.

Donald Neilson – the man accused of being the Black Panther – faces a hostile reception as he arrives at court. Accused of kidnapping and murdering Lesley Whittle, Neilson admitted being responsible for her abduction but denied anything to do with her death. In July 1976 it took the jury just five hours to find him guilty and the Black Panther was sentenced to life imprisonment.

Daily Mirror

EUROPE'S BIGGEST DAILY SALE

Heiress murder charge

PANTHER CASE FURY

Crowd jeer as accused father is led to court

Donald Neilson soon after his arrest for the shotgun murders of three sub-postmasters and the kidnap and murder of heiress Lesley Whittle. He was attacked by members of the public as police struggled with him.

Ben Needham

Ben Needham, aged 21 months old, disappeared on 24th July 1991 on the Greek island of Kos. Despite an intensive manhunt, no trace of the boy nor his kidnapper have ever been found.

A distraught Kerry Needham clings to the hope that her son will be found. Although no ransom demand has ever been made, it is thought that he was possibly "kidnapped to order".

The search for missing Ben Needham continued for more than 20 years. British police hunted for the child's remains in October 2012 after it was suggested that he died in an accident near to where the family were staying in Kos. No trace of him was found and his mother is still convinced that he was kidnapped.

Sarah Payne Sarah Payne's parents make a distraught plea to whoever kidnapped their daughter in July 2000.

Police charge Roy Whiting with the kidnap and murder of schoolgirl Sarah Payne. The case was particularly notable for the extensive use of forensic science in establishing the prosecution case against Whiting, with some 20 experts employed.

"Every parent's nightmare" shouts the headline as it is revealed that Roy Whiting had already been convicted of a previous attack on a schoolgirl. This time, however, the killer was sentenced to serve at least 40 years in prison.

DAILY Mirror
NEWSPAPER OF THE YEAR   60p
Saturday May 5 2007

WHO TOOK OUR MADDY?

Agony as 3-yr-old vanishes from holiday flat

From MARTIN FRICKER in Praia da Luz

A HUGE hunt was going on last night for three-year-old Maddy McCann, feared snatched from her holiday flat.

Madeleine McCann The beginning of a mystery that remains unsolved today. Madeleine McCann disappeared while on holiday in Portugal in May 2007. Numerous theories have been put forward regarding her abduction and potential suspects have been interviewed, but to no avail.

Madeleine's parents, Kate and Gerry McCann, attend a church service as the search for their daughter continues.

An aerial view of the Ocean Club in Praia da Luz, Portugal, where Madeleine McCann went missing.

Suspect Robert Murat and his solicitor Francisco Pagarete in Praia da Luz. He questioned whether the McCanns should still be in Portugal.

Kate McCann leaves Portimão police station in September 2007 after hours of questioning over the disappearance of her daughter.

Shannon Matthews Karen Matthews, mother of missing schoolgirl Shannon Matthews, is pictured with partner Craig Meehan holding a reward poster in March 2008.

Police dog teams from five police forces were involved in the search for Shannon Matthews in Dewsbury.

The bedroom where Shannon Matthews spent her days held by Mick Donovan, in Lidgate Gardens, Batley Carr, West Yorkshire. The room contained a bunk bed, an electronic keyboard, a busted CD, a glue gun and a book (*Arrive Alive*).

There were emotional scenes at Dewsbury Crown Court as Karen Matthews was remanded in custody protected by a heavy police presence.

FISTS, FURY.. AND TEARS IN COURT

▶ April accused breaks down ▶ Crowds hurl abuse

TROLL GETS 12 WEEKS

April Jones The high-profile kidnapping of April Jones from the Welsh market town of Machynlleth sparked nationwide concern in October 2012. Hundreds of volunteers joined the police in their search for the 5-year-old while suspect Mark Bridger appeared in court charged with her murder.

Locals are given search areas in Machynlleth in the hunt for 5-year-old April Jones. Hundreds of people joined the search for April, who was with friends near her Machynlleth home when she got willingly into a van.

Hundreds of lanterns are launched from the Bryn-Y-Gog estate, Machynlleth, in memory of April Jones.

thing is for the authorities to move." Pierre had been kidnapped by two masked men with machine guns as he left his Montreal home on the previous weekend, having planned to go out to dinner with his wife. The ransom's terms included the same demands as did the note for James's safe return.

A "middle-man" who could arrange a deal with terrorists to save the lives of these two hostages was released from a Montreal jail on 12th October 1970. The decision to free 29-year-old lawyer Robert Lemieux sparked off speculation that the Canadian authorities were ready to give in to the kidnappers' main ransom demands. Lemieux was named by terrorists as their go-between to discuss freedom terms for both men. He had been arrested the previous Sunday and charged with obstructing police inquiries into the kidnappings. Known as a sympathizer of the FLQ, he was due to appear in court on 13th October. He would represent several of the 23 jailed FLQ members whose freedom was being demanded. There was speculation that an aircraft would fly the prisoners out of the country to Cuba or Algeria, if the Canadian government gave the go-ahead for their release. The terrorists offered to negotiate over the release of the two hostages and guaranteed that both Cross and Laporte were still alive. The gang also pledged that the two men would be freed 24 hours after the ransom terms were met.

The gang also stopped setting new deadlines for the execution of the two men. The FLQ's offer of talks came in reply to an appeal from Quebec Premier Robert Bourassa, who had hinted that his Cabinet might be ready to negotiate if the kidnappers could prove that the hostages were still alive. As a result, Cross was allowed to send a letter of thanks to Bourassa in which he said: "Thank you for saving my life and that of Mr Laporte. Your humanity in this difficult situation cannot help but be much appreciated by our families." The final decision on whether to give in to the kidnappers would rest with Prime Minister Pierre Trudeau's federal government in Ottawa. Montreal civic leaders had been in a state of flux and were denied protection from the police due to resources being used to safeguard government figures instead. Several families were reported to have left Montreal for a few days until the kidnapping crisis was over. In Quebec, the authorities were criticized for refusing to concede anything to the kidnappers until the eleventh hour. Premier Bourassa's statement came literally minutes before the deadline set for the murder of Laporte ran out. Previously, the federal and provincial governments had flatly refused the terrorists' demands and some observers felt that only the kidnapping of one of the Canadian ministers had forced the authorities to begin softening their line with the terrorists. The next day, 14th October, talks started between two lawyers to secure the release of the two kidnapped men. Lemieux negotiated for the French-Canadian terrorists, while 33-year-old Robert Demers represented the Quebec government. The negotiations took place in the heavily guarded jail in Montreal, while at the same time about 400 troops arrived in Ottawa in helicopters and trucks to help hard-pressed police in guarding federal Cabinet Ministers and other likely kidnap targets. Some troops were put on duty inside the parliament building, but were later withdrawn after an MP described their presence as "revolting".

Lemieux appeared happy and relaxed to be representing the FLQ, an underground left-wing group that had been in operation since 1963. Accused of all sorts of criminal activities, including bombings and murder, the FLQ had been responsible for a terror campaign in their struggle to set up Quebec as an independent "French" state within Canada. Six people had already died as a result of the organization's terrorist activities. However, Lemieux's view was that the terrorist crimes, violent as they may have been, were basically protests against the oppression of French Canadians by what he called the "pigs" of the establishment. More than 80 per cent of Quebec's six million population were French-speaking at that time. The lawyer had ended his own links with the establishment three years earlier, when he quit his job with an old established Montreal law firm. Despite his close connections with the FLQ, Lemieux claimed he had had no contact with the kidnappers during the eight-day police search for the hostages, but he was known as the only man whom the terrorist group could trust. However, as negotiations got under way, the terrorists set a new deadline for the execution of their two hostages.

Troops in Ottawa were mirrored by troops in Montreal on 15th October when they moved into the centre of the country's kidnapping crisis to guard public buildings and prominent figures. There were rumours that the police knew the whereabouts of Laporte, but were waiting to discover where envoy Cross was being held before moving in. The terrorists said they would execute both men should the police close in. Meanwhile, there was a growing feeling that the Canadian government would declare a state of emergency in an all-out attempt to find the kidnappers and their victims. The move would enable police to search buildings without warrants and to hold people for questioning without charging them. On 16th October 1970, Trudeau decided on drastic action and nearly 250 people were seized in dawn raids across Quebec province. In its most ruthless crackdown at that time on the terrorists, the government put into force the War Measures Act, which gave the police almost unlimited powers. At the same time, the French-Canadian terrorist organization was outlawed. Any person belonging to the FLQ or even being connected with it could now be jailed for five years. As 14,000 police and soldiers were mobilized, there was strong criticism of the government for introducing "panic measures". Fears mounted that the immediate result would be the execution of the two hostages. The leader of the oppositional New Democratic Party, Tommy Douglas, said: "Canadians will look back on this as the Black Friday of Civil Liberties" and added that the Liberal government were "using a sledgehammer to crack a peanut". Speculation grew that the authorities had discovered the hideouts where the hostages were being held and were preparing a swoop. The arrests came in four cities: Montreal, Quebec City, Rimouski and Chicoutimi. Known supporters of the FLQ were hauled from their beds and bundled into waiting police cars, and stockpiles of arms were seized. One of the first to be picked up was Robert Lemieux, only hours before he had angrily rejected the government's "final offer" of the release of five prisoners. A grim-faced Trudeau told the federal parliament that he was invoking the War Measures Act with "deep regret". The fate of the two kidnapped men weighed heavily on his mind, he said, and added: "A violent revolution is seeking the destruction of social order."

On 18th October it was revealed that James Cross was still alive. However, Pierre Laporte had been found brutally murdered in the bloodstained boot of a car. According to reports, he had been shot in the head. His wrists had been slashed and he was found in the same car that had been used to kidnap him. After the gruesome find, weeping men and women prayed in churches across Canada that James Cross would not meet a similar fate. A call came from the terrorists to a radio station to say where the note – proving James was still alive – could be found. In it he said how the incorrect news on the television earlier that day – stating that he was also dead – must have been terrible news for his wife. He went on to say: "I am alive and well. My life is not threatened for the moment." In a communiqué accompanying the note, the terrorists once again repeated their demands and said that James would be executed if they weren't met. A shamed Premier Trudeau invited the kidnappers to the Concordia Bridge across the St Lawrence River, where they could release James Cross in return for their own freedom and a flight to Cuba. In order to make the kidnappers feel absolutely secure, the 400-yard bridge was temporarily designated as Cuban territory.

Pierre Laporte was found dead after a call to a radio station that led the police to the Place des Artes cultural centre in Montreal. Here they found a crudely drawn map and a note saying that Mr Laporte had been executed. Guided by the map, the police went to an airbase near Montreal where they discovered the car near a fence outside a hangar. It was more than five hours before the boot was opened as police feared that the car might have been booby-trapped. An army bomb-disposal unit was called in and finally prised open the boot and pulled away a bloodstained sheet. Mr Laporte lay face up with his hands folded across his chest. The last letter the victim ever wrote – to Bourassa – stated: "Decide – it's my life or my death. I'm counting on you." His family – wife Francoise, his 21-year-old daughter, Claire, and 13-year-old son, Jean – were left devastated.

Rene Laporte, mother of the victim, was forced to share her private grief with a nation, comforted by relatives, as she left the building in which she had just seen her dead son. Mrs Laporte was one of the first mourners to see her son lying in state. A massive security guard surrounded the funeral of Pierre on 20th October 1970. But, as Canada mourned, there was still no word of James Cross. Strict security measures were set up as the authorities feared reprisals from the FLQ after the government turned down their ransom demands. Despite more than 1,600 police raids across Quebec, the kidnappers of James Cross and the murderers of Pierre Laporte had still not been found.

Just two days after the funeral of Pierre Laporte, his macabre execution was described for the first time. He had been strangled with a slim gold chain that hung around his neck carrying a religious medallion. He was still wearing the chain when his body was found. Marks on his neck showed that he had been strangled from behind in a classic commando style. The way in which this hostage had died sent a new wave of horror through the Canadian people, who were already stunned and disgusted by the cold-blooded killing. The coroner, Laurin Lapointe, dispelled the rumours that Laporte had been shot. There were cuts on the Minister's chest, wrist and hands that indicated he had possibly been tortured by the gang.

On 23rd October, just three days after Pierre Laporte's funeral, Canadian jet fighter-bombers joined in the hunt for James Cross. The jets combed the southern half of the province of Quebec with aerial cameras filming the countryside below. The films were then rushed to the military base at Bagotville, Quebec, where intelligence officers examined them for signs of unusual activity on farmland and remote areas. For two weeks, there was no news.

In early November, experts were said to be studying a dramatic photograph of a man who could have been James Cross. The photograph sent to police showed the man sitting on a box marked "explosives" calmly playing patience. The police then tried to establish whether the photo was genuine, or whether it had been sent by the FLQ. By this time, James Cross had been missing for nearly five weeks and nothing had been heard from him or his kidnappers since he sent a note on 18th October saying: "I am alive". Meanwhile, just three days after the photo arrived, on 10th November, 19-year-old Montreal student Bernard Lortie was being held by police. He had confessed to being one of four men who kidnapped Pierre Laporte and was also able to give them information about the kidnapping of James Cross. After 59 days in captivity James Cross was on the verge of freedom, following a harrowing journey in a car booby-trapped with dynamite in case the police tried to arrest the kidnappers on the journey. He was driven in a 20-car motorcade from the kidnappers' hideout in a Montreal suburb to an island in the St Lawrence River. There, from the Canadian Pavilion on the Expo 67 site, he telephoned Bourassa to say: "I feel fine, and I'm in good shape. But, this is the first time in eight weeks that I have seen the sun." At first it was thought that James Cross would be freed when he reached St Helen's island, but then came a snag. The kidnappers – Marc Carbonneau and Jacques Lanctot – demanded safe conduct to Cuba for their families. They had already been granted safe conduct for themselves in exchange for Mr Cross's freedom. Two hours after they all arrived at the island, their new demand was still being discussed. It seemed that the demand was granted, as the kidnappers' families were collected. The kidnappers were driven to Montreal international airport, escorted by Cuban diplomat Ricardo Escartin, where they were to be flown by military plane to Havana. As soon as James Cross was freed, he called his wife, Barbara, in Berne, Switzerland.

After eight weeks in darkness in a terrorist hideout, James Cross had lost 22lbs. He woke up on 4th December 1970 in Montreal's Jewish General Hospital to a cooked breakfast as snow was falling across the city. "I feel great", he told doctors, and asked when he might go home. It was expected that he would fly to Britain following his ordeal, where he would be reunited with his wife. A "deliriously happy" Mrs Cross told the *Daily Mirror* how her husband had watched 162 French films on TV while in captivity, which had greatly improved his French. She went on to say: "He didn't speak very much to the kidnappers, who gave him lots of revolutionary literature. He was guarded day and night by two men with sub-machine guns." Meanwhile, the kidnappers and their families landed in Havana.

Cross told of "the most terrible night of my life" that came when he saw a television announcement of his own death while he was being held by the kidnappers. Reliving the agonizing moment at a press conference in London on 9th December, he said: "I feared my wife had seen the announcement." He revealed that he was kept in handcuffs for the first two weeks and that he was made to wear a hood at all times. He often thought about trying to escape from the windowless room where he was held, but decided against it. "I felt that the odds were against me – that I would be shot dead or confined again in absolutely impossible conditions", he said. He also revealed that he had never been allowed to see his captors, who only spoke to him behind his head. There had been five kidnappers in total, four men and one woman, who only spoke to him in French. He admitted that there were times when he sank into "complete despair". At the end of December 1970, three of the main suspects in the Canadian kidnappings were arrested at an apparently empty farmhouse after a light was spotted. Paul Rose, a

27-year-old teacher, his brother Jacques, and Francis Simard, both aged 23, were all arrested at the farmhouse. A fourth unidentified man was also arrested. A tip-off on Christmas Day had led police to the remote spot and the house was stormed. It appeared empty, but four days later they found three men hidden in a dug-out beneath the cellar. The entrance to the hideaway, behind a furnace in the basement, was only 14in sq. Meanwhile, in January 1971, it was revealed that James Cross had been given an unprecedented amount of money. It is believed that the £20,000 he received as an ex-gratia payment was for the mental and physical hardships he had endured during his weeks in captivity and the fact that he had refused all publishing deals (some said to be in the region of £80,000) due to being bound as a senior civil servant. Despite the fact that any book or article would have been about personal endurance rather than about life in the civil service, it must have still come as a relief to the Foreign Office – to whom he was assigned while in Canada – that James Cross chose to keep his story private. The major criticism against the Canadian government was that they had used Cross as a political pawn. The accusation was that Trudeau saw the kidnappings as an excuse to crush the terrorists, so he brought in troops and launched a major anti-terrorist drive without caring for the fate of the British envoy. As the *Daily Mirror* wrote in January 1971, Cross was "justly compensated after a harrowing experience", and was further honoured when the Queen invested him with the Order of St Michael and St George in February that same year.

Patty Hearst

(1974)

American newspaper heiress Patricia (Patty) Hearst was kidnapped by an armed gang at the beginning of February 1974. The 20-year-old granddaughter of the late newspaper tycoon William Randolph Hearst was believed to have been snatched by what was then a new-style group of revolutionaries called the Symbionese Liberation Army. She was taken when a gang of two men and a woman broke into her flat in Berkeley, California. Police kept the kidnapping a secret for 12 hours in the hope that the gang would contact her millionaire father, Randolph Hearst, then chairman of the huge newspaper chain. The university student was tied up, blindfolded and taken half-naked to a car. Two men fired shots at passers-by who came running after hearing Patty's screams, but no one was hurt.

Hopes for the release of Patty rose on 17th February after her family received a tape recording of her voice. She said that she was not being beaten or starved. She told her father: "Whatever you come up with basically is okay. Just do it as fast as you can, and everything will be fine." It was also confirmed that the new revolutionary group were indeed holding the heiress. They gave her father until 18th February to start handing out free food to the poor in California, threatening that they would kill his daughter if he did not comply. Randolph Hearst maintained that he could not afford to meet the cost of the operation, which could have run into millions of pounds, and said he would come up with a "counter-offer". In the seven-minute tape, collected from a luggage locker in San Francisco after a phone call to a clergyman, Patty said her captors realized that their demand could not be met. She said: "It was never intended that he should feed the whole state". She also pleaded with the FBI not to try to free her. "I think I can get out of here alive as long as the FBI don't come busting in", she said. However, a life-or-death ultimatum was about to ensue.

On 22nd February 1974 a mob rioted as they waited for a ransom of free food to be handed over by Randolph Hearst's publishing firm to the gang of kidnappers. The crowd, who had been queuing for hours, attacked a lorry delivering supplies to a distribution centre at Oakland, near San Francisco. Hurling rocks and bottles, they dragged the driver from his cab, while looters escaped with some of the food (and a TV camera). Most of the food was trampled underfoot by the 15,000-strong crowd. Several people were hurt as police stormed the mainly black area and Mr Hearst's company gave the kidnappers an ultimatum. The firm agreed that they would meet the kidnappers' new demand for an extra food ransom for the poor of £1,600,000 in two instalments, but only if Patty was released unharmed. They also made it perfectly clear to the gang that no further payments would be made "under any circumstances". The company revealed its "get tough" policy with the terrorists when Randolph Hearst read out an emotional statement at his home just outside San Francisco. Mr Hearst also made it clear that in trying to save his daughter he had run out of money. "The size of the latest demand is far beyond my financial capabilities", he said. "Therefore the matter is now out of my hands." But then Charles Gould, publisher of the Hearst Corporation's *San Francisco Examiner*, stepped in and said that the company was prepared to contribute half of the latest demand immediately, providing Patty was released unharmed. The rest of the money would be paid the following January, he stated. The Hearst family then faced the agony of waiting.

Meanwhile, in another kidnapping, the gang who snatched editor Reg Murphy (also in February 1974) promised to release him on a ransom of £280,000. The promise came in a telephone call from a self-styled colonel in the American Revolutionary Army, a right-wing group. Officials of the editor's Georgia paper, the *Atlanta Constitution*, had agreed to pay and confirmed that the kidnappers had picked up the money. Murphy was eventually freed after 49 hours by his captor, William Williams, in a Ramada Inn parking lot. Williams was then arrested just six hours later and all the money recovered. Despite Williams saying he was part of a huge revolutionary gang, it appeared that the father of two had been acting alone. He was sentenced to 40 years in jail, but served nine, and, following the trauma, Reg Murphy went back to his life.

On 3rd April 1974, it was claimed that Patty Hearst would be staying with the gang who had kidnapped her. The claim was made on a tape recording delivered to a San Francisco radio station, allegedly by a member of the gang. On the tape, a man identifying himself as a field marshal in the "army" said: "The prisoner is now a comrade." The tape dashed hopes that the 20-year-old student would be reunited with her family – and more drama was yet to come. In mid-April Patty Hearst went from being searched for, to being wanted by the FBI. She was pictured on a hidden camera, holding a gun during a bank robbery. What wasn't known was whether she was a bank robber of her own free will, or had been coerced into raiding the bank by her kidnappers. A hidden security camera had identified Patty as one of the robbers when she and three other women and a man walked into a San Francisco bank armed with sten-guns. The gang escaped with £4,000, firing random shots as they fled and wounding two passers-by.

There had been some speculation about whether Patty was involved in the kidnap plot from the start, but her parents maintained that she had been brainwashed during her captivity. In early May 1974 police found the hideout used by the kidnappers, but it was empty. Terrorist slogans were scrawled on the walls of the San Francisco apartment, which the gang were believed to have left just five days earlier on 30th April. Some of the slogans were signed "Tania", the name taken by Patty when she announced that she had joined the gang who kidnapped her, while clothing used in the bank raid by the gang was discovered. A key was also found which fitted a hire car used in the raid and later found abandoned nearby. A neighbour of the property identified a picture of the gang's leader, escaped convict Donald de Freeze. She said that he had lived in the three-room apartment since the middle of March and often bought food at a local supermarket. The hideout was discovered when neighbours complained about cockroaches spreading from the filthy, abandoned apartment.

Later in May 1974, Patty Hearst was being branded by the FBI as "armed and dangerous" and a warrant was issued for her arrest. She was on the run with two "soldiers" of the Symbionese Liberation Army (SLA) – William Harris, 29, and his wife Emily, 27 – who, alongside the heiress, faced charges of kidnapping and armed robbery. The new twist in Patty's story came in an announcement from the FBI in Los Angeles. They said that Patty and the Harris couple had gone to Mel's Sporting Store in Inglewood, Los Angeles, where Emily Harris was buying clothing worth about £15 when shop assistants saw her husband putting a pair of socks (worth about 20 pence) up his jacket sleeve. William Harris was challenged, guns were drawn, and the FBI said that Patty, who was outside the shop, opened fire with an automatic rifle. The trio got away in a stolen van, taking the driver, 18-year-old Tom Matthews, as a hostage. He was held for 12 hours as they drove around. Tom Matthews said that all three had told him they were members of the SLA, and Patty said that she had been part of the San Francisco bank robbery. The frightened young man said Patty was referred to as "Tania" and that she had a loaded automatic weapon.

Police then began a helicopter search for Patty Hearst. They searched the rugged canyons north of Beverly Hills after a man claimed to have spoken to the three fugitives. The FBI were convinced that Patty voluntarily joined the gang. Retired army sergeant William Walls told FBI agents that he had spoken to the three outside his home in a remote canyon, but they had driven off after he refused to put them up for the night. Four months after her kidnapping, the heiress decided to disclose why she had joined the gang. She said that she became one of the gang because she was "disappointed" in her family's efforts to get her freed.

While still on the run, she told her story to Tom Matthews. He said that she told him she had played no part in her own kidnapping, but she had decided to join the terrorists because she felt that her father had not done enough to meet the ransom demands. However, her distraught parents, Randolph and Catherine, told newspapers that "no matter what she says, we still love her". In one of the tape recordings sent to the family Patty told of her love for one of her kidnappers, which perhaps provided the biggest clue at the time as to why she had switched from being the victim to one of the gang. It was also at this time that the police believed they had found Patty at a terrorist hideout in Los Angeles. In a bloody shoot-out, all six terrorists were killed, but Patty was not among them. By March 1975, the young heiress was still on the run and missing.

Patty Hearst was eventually arrested on 18th September 1975. FBI agents grabbed her in a house only a few hundred yards from the headquarters of her newspaper tycoon father. The FBI also arrested three of Patty's fellow guerillas, including William and Emily Harris and a woman called Wendy Yoshimura. All four gave in without a struggle. The peaceful end to the Patty Hearst saga conflicted with her previously defiant statement a few months before that: "I will not be taken alive". The terrorist group were driven off in handcuffs in two cars and a few hours later Patty made a brief appearance in the Federal Court in San Francisco, facing charges that included bank robbery. She made no comment, and was remanded in custody with bail set at £500,000. William and Emily Harris were next in the dock, where the prosecutor said they faced charges in connection with America's Firearms Act. While Emily Harris remained silent, her husband raised clenched fists and declared: "My comrades keep on truckin'. This ain't no big deal." The three were to appear in court again on the afternoon of 19th September. Randolph Hearst was in New York when he heard a radio news bulletin that his daughter had been arrested. He contacted his wife, Catherine, in Los Angeles where she was attending a meeting. Speaking on behalf of Mrs Hearst, her friend Carolyn Fax said that when Catherine hung up the phone she simply said: "They found Patty." She looked relieved, but shaken.

Patty's astonishing switch in 1975 from wealthy socialite to gun-toting urban guerilla was one of the most bizarre puzzles the FBI had ever faced. Patty's parents couldn't bring themselves to believe that their daughter had renounced her background of her own free will, but the FBI had no doubts. The arrests had come about when they received a tip-off that Patty had stayed at a secluded farmhouse in Harrisburg, Pennsylvania, in the summer of 1974. They found evidence of Patty's presence at the house and traced her back to San Francisco. Two sets of fingerprints at the farmhouse had led to her arrest. The FBI had concentrated on tracing Wendy

Yoshimura – who had also stayed at the farmhouse for a short time that summer – and they questioned all her known friends and acquaintances. The hunt took them to Stephen Soliah, who earlier in September 1975 rented a flat in the name of Charles Adams in Morse Street, a seedy area of San Francisco. It was this flat that the FBI raided and where they would eventually find Patty. The charges of kidnapping and bank robbery meant that the heiress was possibly facing a life sentence. In court, she gave her occupation as "urban guerilla", while her father made arrangements to raise the bail money. Despite the fact that Patty had called her parents "fascist pigs" in a tape recording in 1974, they took a bouquet of yellow roses to jail when they visited her and afterwards they told reporters how well the meeting had gone and that their daughter wanted to come home. Randolph Hearst was fairly optimistic about his daughter's future. He said: "I don't think anything will happen. After all, she was a kidnap victim."

"Patty Hearst publicly and viciously denounced all that her rich, socially prominent family stands for", wrote Marje Proops in the *Daily Mirror*. "The world eavesdropped on her declaration that she regarded her father as a Fascist pig", she continued, yet her parents' reaction to Patty's capture was "predictable", states Proops. They reacted just like almost every other parent would in similar circumstances. "Call it a rescue", said her mother, "not a capture." To the mother and father whose lifestyle Patty had so scorned, wrote Proops, their revolutionary daughter now wanted to go home. She goes on to write how Mrs Hearst acted as though her daughter was still the same girl she was before the kidnapping. "She isn't of course", states the journalist – not after living for almost two years as a fugitive with revolutionary companions. But to her mother she was the same child wanting to go home. Proops finishes the article by saying: "For whatever terrible things children do to bring grief, disappointment and even shame to their mothers and fathers, there aren't many parents who would fail to welcome back the prodigal child. Forgiving scornful insults, forgetting the pain and the rejection; just thankful to have them back at any price. That's what being a parent is really all about."

Patty's lawyers claimed that she was "driven to the brink of insanity by her captors". She was quoted in a sworn statement as saying that she "lived in a fog" during her ordeal. Patty told that after having been dragged half-naked from the arms of her boyfriend Stephen Weed – who was badly beaten at the time of the kidnap – she was imprisoned in a cupboard for nine weeks. She was given no food and was "unable to dispose of her body waste". Later, the terrorists who seized her had forced her to join them in a bank raid. In court, Patty Hearst was facing 22 charges and three psychiatrists were asked to decide if she was fit to face questioning.

In October 1975, newspapers reported how Patty had been keen to prove to her captors how liberated she was – especially where sex was concerned. According to documents seized by the FBI, it is alleged that she was so enthusiastic about group sex that her captors thought she was faking something in order to cover up escape plans. At first her kidnappers argued about whether it was correct for members of the "army" to have sex with a "prisoner of war" in case she later claimed she had been raped. But Patty, whom they nicknamed Tania, quickly made it clear that she would be an eager participant. The documents were found in the San Francisco house where William and Emily Harris were captured. One paper, apparently written by Emily Harris, said: "It was only natural that with increased personal interaction between Tania and members of the cell these relationships would develop sexually. Some comrades feared the pigs might say we raped her. However, Tania swiftly made it clear to us that this could not be the case."

In March 1976, newspapers were asking: "Patty Hearst – gun-toting terrorist or terrified victim?" This was the issue facing the jury of seven women and five men. Was she, as federal prosecutor James Browning argued, their willing accomplice? Or, did she, as the defence counsel F Lee Bailey maintained, join up with them in fear for her life? Bailey had summed up the defence in two dramatic sentences. He told the jury: "We all have a covenant with death and we all try to postpone it as long as possible. Patty Hearst tried to do that." There were two kinds of kidnap victims, he said – those who lived and those who died. "The ones who survive do exactly what they are told." He added slowly: "As you would and I would." But prosecutor Browning claimed: "The story is just too incredible to believe. It is just too big a pill to swallow. It just doesn't wash." The jury who had sat through the eight-week trial were expected to deliver their verdict on 21st March. Patty was facing a 25-year jail sentence if found guilty.

The bond between Patty Hearst and 27-year-old US federal marshal Janey Jiminez became apparent when the verdict was read out. The marshal had been a constant companion for Patty as she was escorted to and from the courtroom. When the "guilty" verdict was announced, Janey wept openly. However, despite the verdict, Patty was said to be in fear of her life from the terrorists who kidnapped her. The accusations she had made from the witness stand against her fellow terrorists marked her for vengeance. The fact that two Hearst family properties were bombed during the 40-day trial showed that the movement was still active. Patty had been found guilty of voluntarily joining the terrorists in the San Francisco bank raid. However, she still had to face a further trial in Los Angeles on charges of kidnapping, robbery and assault. There was speculation that she might "go free" if she gave evidence against the Harris couple. But, Patty was well aware this could put her in grave danger. Her lawyers claimed that a jail sentence could also become a death sentence for Patty. They asked Judge Oliver Carter to give her probation for her part in the bank robbery. It was reported that since the seven months she had been in custody Patty had lost weight, was depressed and could not eat or sleep properly. When the heiress was given a provisional 55-year jail sentence, her lawyer applied for a new trial for the bank robbery charges. In 1976 she was eventually given seven years in jail for the robbery – one of which she had already served since her arrest in 1975. In December 1976 she claimed that her bank-raid gun had been phony: "It was explained to me before I was forced to go on the raid that the bolt was open and the gun wouldn't fire." At this point, Patty Hearst was free on bail and talking for the first time about her kidnapping. She showed no pity for her six terrorist comrades who died in the shoot-out with police and stated: "They all got exactly what they deserved." She didn't, however, mention William Wolf, the gang member with whom she had had a love affair and who died in the battle with police. Her comments, given in an exclusive television interview, were expected to infuriate terrorist sympathizers who had sworn to kill her for co-operating with the authorities. In December 1976, safe inside the Hearst family ranch estate, Patty looked much happier than she had done in more than two years. On 9th May 1977 she was given five years probation for her part in the armed robbery: she had managed to hang on to her freedom. The light sentence surprised many lawyers because she had sprayed a crowded street with machine-gun fire, but no one had been hurt. The judge, Talbot Callister, maintained that the light sentence came out of consideration for Patty's parents and the fact that both defence and the prosecution had asked for probation. At this time, Patty was still appealing the seven-year jail sentence for the robbery of the San Francisco bank.

In November 1977, it was reported that Patty Hearst was seeing policeman Bernard Shaw, 30, who had been "moonlighting" for $10 an hour as one of her bodyguards. But, in May 1978 she was back in prison when it was announced that she would have to serve the rest of the seven-year sentence. Her appeal had been rejected. It was expected that the US Justice Department would recommend her release and that a pardon from US President, Jimmy Carter, would be forthcoming. She was freed in January 1979 and married Shaw in April that same year. In 1981, Patty gave birth to a daughter. However, the story didn't end there.

Writing in her autobiography *Every Secret Thing* in 1981, Patty Hearst described how she drove the getaway car in a bank robbery in which a woman was murdered. She was given immunity after giving vital information about the murder gang to police. She also revealed that she blew up two police cars with bombs in San Francisco during her time with the kidnapping gang, but she was sued for £3.5 million over her account of her kidnap by terrorists. The book says that Jack and Micki Scott, from Portland, Oregon, actively helped the terrorists by operating a secret transport system, but the couple said that they helped Patty because they wanted to stop her joining the guerillas in an assassination attempt. Mrs Scott claimed that the heiress libeled them in her book and that she was "the one who most often talked of killing people".

Patty and her husband Bernard Shaw gave an interview to Paul Callan writing for the *Daily Mirror* in April 1982, accompanied by their 10-month-old daughter, Gillian. The world was told – in Patty's book – how she was no longer a terrorist or a mixed-up spoiled rich girl. "She had been the victim of brainwashing." Callan writes: "Patty seems remarkably untouched by the horror of those days" and she says herself: "But my life is so different now, what happened then seems so distant. If I have been psychologically affected, I certainly don't feel it." According to the newspaper article, Patty had been "kidnapped, raped, brainwashed and jailed – but now [she] is so happy again". "This", says Patricia (as she's called in most of the interview), "is the happiest time of my life. I don't want to change it." By 1989, Patty had emerged from her private hell. She was a millionairess, a suburban socialite and happily married with two young daughters. She was a successful author and the film *Patty Hearst*, the graphic portrayal of her kidnap and subsequent two years as part of the "army" and time on the FBI's most wanted list, was about to hit the silver screen. It was more than 10 years since Patty had been snatched. Her parents divorced due to the stress of the two-year ordeal, and the remainder of the SLA were living respectable lives. William Harris became a private eye. Emily changed her name and moved into obscurity. Another woman ran a fruit-juice bar on the Berkeley university campus where it had all begun. Asked if she would go along with the terrorists if she were kidnapped again, Patty Hearst exclaimed: "I'd rather be dead."

Lesley Whittle

(1975)

The mother of kidnap heiress Lesley Whittle waited anxiously for a vital message on 15th January 1975. Beside Dorothy Whittle throughout her agonizing vigil was a bag containing £50,000 in used notes. The call she expected was from the kidnapper of her daughter. Seventeen-year-old Lesley had been snatched from her Shropshire home and the kidnapper had demanded a £50,000 ransom by one o'clock – the day that Dorothy was waiting for the message. If it was not paid, the girl would die, he said.

Early on 16th January, Lesley's brother, Ronald, 31, waited in a phone box. He was hoping that Lesley's kidnapper would contact him. The story of the ransom drama was revealed by the man leading the hunt for Lesley, Detective Chief Superintendent Bob Booth. The kidnap message had been written on red plastic tape. Part of it said: "Only after £50,000 has been cleared will the victim be released." DCS Booth said that members of the Whittle family had got the money in used £1 and £5 notes on the day of the kidnap. He added: "There was nothing they would not have done to get their daughter back." He said that the kidnappers might have changed their plans when they heard news of the kidnap on television. Breaking the news of the kidnap might well have put Lesley's life in danger, he added. Police interviewed Lesley's boyfriend, university student Richard Forder, whom they later cleared from their inquiries.

Lesley and Richard had been going out for just over a year, having met at Wulfrun College in Wolverhampton where they were both students. They had spent the weekend before the kidnap together, and on the night before the kidnap had slept at Richard's parents' home in Wombourne Park, near Wolverhampton.

Police then made a special search for jewellery that Lesley was known to have been wearing when she was kidnapped – she had vanished barefoot wearing only a blue dressing gown. It was also revealed that she had been left £82,000 by her father, wealthy coach manufacturer George Whittle, but it was known that the money was in trust. Lesley's friends then told reporters that she had kept her family's wealth a secret.

However, despite a desperate vigil at the telephone box named by the kidnappers on their ransom note, the phone didn't ring on Tuesday or Wednesday at the kiosk in Kidderminster, Worcester. Meanwhile, a "search everything" sweep of the area around Lesley's home in Highley, Shropshire, was underway by police. On 22nd January 1975, Dorothy Whittle made a heartbroken plea to her daughter's kidnappers. She said: "For God's sake end this terrible agony of silence. Let me know something – even if it is that Lesley is dead." The desperate appeal went out from 55-year-old widow, Dorothy, as she spent her eighth day by the telephone waiting for instructions about delivering the £50,000 ransom. By this time, police feared that the young woman had been murdered, but Dorothy Whittle said: "I only wish the people involved could see what they are putting me through. The waiting is the worst part. I just sit helpless hoping for the phone to ring."

In the following days, police suspected that Lesley's family were secretly negotiating with the kidnappers for her release. Her brother Ron told reporters on 27th January that the family were happy with the way that the police were carrying out their investigation, but he stated: "There is a conflict of priorities. They want to get Lesley back and capture the kidnappers. My priority is the safe return of my sister." Ron Whittle was prepared to go anywhere at any time to meet the kidnappers on his own without telling the police. Detectives thought he had already been in touch with them, but was keeping his communication with the gang a secret. So far, the police had found no trace of the missing teenager and were worried about the family's secret negotiations. It completely went against all advice they had given the Whittle family – and DCS Bob Booth was convinced that Lesley was in the hands of "a ruthless gang".

By 11th February 1975, it was known that Lesley had been taken by the most wanted man in Britain – the Black Panther – a triple killer branded as the most dangerous criminal at large in the country. The sensational revelation was made by top detectives who were convinced that the gunman was the same man who was wanted for the murders of three sub-postmasters. Known to wear a black hood with narrow eye slits, the Black Panther talked to his victims in short, staccato bursts. His other trademark was his ruthlessness. At the slightest hint of resistance, he was liable to shoot to kill. The Post Office and the National Federation of Sub-Postmasters had already put up a £25,000 reward for the capture of the Panther. He was known to speak with a Black Country accent and was thought to live in the Midlands. Detectives believed he worked as a long-distance lorry driver or travelling salesman. As the Whittle family owned a successful coach business, police were sure that the gunman had picked up information about the family during his travels, which is what prompted and helped his plan of kidnapping Lesley.

More than a dozen clues, which it was hoped would trap the killer, were found by police in the car used to kidnap Lesley. These included false number plates and an excise licence stolen in Leicestershire the month Lesley was snatched from her home. Detectives revealed how they had linked the kidnapping to the Black Panther after they made a breakthrough in the case when a stolen car, used by the kidnapper, was found abandoned in Dudley, Worcestershire. It was in a car park near a freightliner depot where security guard, Gerald Smith, was shot and wounded two nights after the kidnapping. Inside the car was evidence linking the kidnapper with the murder of the three sub-postmasters during the previous 12 months. The dramatic disclosures were made when senior detectives from several forces held a news conference in Dudley. They had established that the gunman snatched Lesley from her home and drove off in a stolen Morris 1300. The car was found abandoned just 150 yards from the spot where Gerald Smith had surprised an intruder and was shot seven times.

Inside the car were a number of red plastic Dymo tapes like the one used for the £50,000 ransom "note" left at Lesley's home. The tapes all bore ransom instructions for rendezvous points throughout the Midlands – including the depot where the security guard was gunned down. Police were also thought to have recovered Lesley's slippers from the kidnap car. There was also a tape recorder and, while the tape that accompanied it was clean, it was thought that the kidnapper had intended Lesley to record a message for her family. Detectives also found a foam mattress on which the victim probably lay while she was held captive, and barley sugar and Lucozade that the gunman must have given to her. The Panther had already netted around £12,000 from his deathly raids on post offices in the north of England and the Midlands since 1971. He had killed three innocent men in cold blood. Donald Skepper died at his post office in Harrogate, Yorkshire, while Derek Astin was killed in Accrington, Lancashire. The third victim was Sydney Grayland who was shot dead at his post office in Langley, Worcestershire, while his wife, Peggy, was battered about the head and left for dead.

The next vital clue in the case came when scientific tests carried out on the car gave police a clear lead in how the kidnapper usually made a living – and a team of 50 detectives were ordered to make nationwide inquiries among people in the same line of work. However, five weeks after the kidnap, the Lesley Whittle case became a murder hunt when her body was recovered from a drain at a beauty spot in Kidsgrove, Staffordshire on 2nd March 1975. The 17-year-old had been strangled with a piece of wire and dumped.

Leading the investigation into Lesley's brutal murder was Commander John Morrison of Scotland Yard. The first question he faced was: did the Black Panther kill this young victim? The police had maintained that there were links between Lesley's kidnap and the killings carried out by the Black Panther, but the chief detectives of three counties involved in the investigation were by no means agreed that it was the Panther who snatched the young woman from her home and then murdered her in cold blood. Commander Morrison faced the difficult task of finding out from these senior officers just what their exact feelings and findings were. Two vital details – it came to light – had never been satisfactorily explained. What was the connection between the stolen car and the killing of the sub-postmasters? And, what was the connection between the car and Lesley's kidnap? There had been suggestions that ballistic evidence linked the car with the post office murders and it had also been mooted that there was evidence to show Lesley had been in the car. However, no one had really said what the evidence was. It was, at this stage, still possible that the Black Panther had committed all four murders, but it was just as likely that the police would have to redirect their hunt for an entirely different person. Lesley's body had been found just yards from where her brother Ron had tried to keep a meeting with her kidnapper and there were clues that the kidnapper had waited for him. Ron Whittle, however, had been late and the meeting never took place. The grim discovery of Lesley's body was made in the early evening as 75 policemen combed Bathpool Park in Kidsgrove with 20 dogs. A manhole cover was lifted from the top of a drain and police saw her body lying in a pool of water. It was believed that Lesley's body had been in the drain for some time. It was then revealed that an amazing game of double bluff had been played with the kidnapper. Ron Whittle had pretended to make a secret deal with the kidnapper, while in actual fact, the police knew about it all along and he had been acting on strict police instructions. A senior officer confirmed that when Ron had tried to keep a meeting with the kidnapper, he was acting under "operational control of the police". Fred Hodges, West Mercia's Assistant Chief Constable, admitted that DCS Bob Booth had been play-acting for television crews and reporters, pretending he knew nothing of Ron Whittle's dealings with the kidnapper, but he said: "It must be brought to public notice that throughout the whole of this difficult inquiry and protracted investigation, the family of Lesley Whittle, and particularly Ronald Whittle, have acted under the guidance and control of the police." He continued: "Any statements so made by Mr Whittle or the police were done so in an attempt to instill confidence in the kidnapper, with the fervent hope that Lesley was still alive and could be returned safely to her family." So what went wrong with the police bluff?

Ron had received a tape-recorded message from his sister over the phone telling him to go to a certain park. However, he got lost on the way and was late for the meeting. The evidence showing that the kidnapper had waited for him included a tape, which was later found by two schoolboys, saying that the money "should be put down the hole". Journalist Tom Tullett, chief of the Mirror Crime Bureau wrote: "Two days before Lesley Whittle's body was found, I asked Superintendent Clifford Taylor if he knew that Ronald Whittle had arranged to meet the kidnapper three days after the kidnap." The police claimed that they did not know.

Lesley Whittle had been dragged from her bed at gunpoint as her family slept. Her family never saw the 17-year-old alive again. It had been some hours before Dorothy Whittle had discovered that her daughter was missing. Wrapped around a vase in the lounge was a piece of red plastic tape several feet long. Punched out on it was the chilling ransom note. The two schoolboys had found the tape message weeks before they handed it to the police, having kept it among their toys. They also handed in a torch they had found on wasteland in Kidsgrove. It led to a culvert in Bathpool Park, which ended 52 days of waiting but led to final heartbreak for the Whittle family.

It was revealed a week later that Lesley had died of sheer terror. As her kidnapper pinioned her arms behind her back with wire and then wound more wire around her throat, the unimaginable horror of it all had been too much for her. In the clammy darkness of an underground shaft, her heart and her whole nervous system just broke down. Death was instantaneous. The cause of her death was revealed by Commander Morrison who said: "A post-mortem examination showed Lesley died of vagal inhibition – her heart stopped through shock." The killer then pushed her off a ledge in the 60ft shaft under Bathpool Park. It was thought that the killer had hoped that the wire, which was attached to a rung of an inspection ladder, would break, which meant that Lesley's body would have eventually floated away. However, the wire held and the young victim's naked body was still hanging by it when she was found. Police believed at this time that the Black Panther was a sewer builder who may have helped to build the Bathpool Park tunnels. By this time, Commander Morrison was convinced that Lesley's killer was the Black Panther. There had been a sewer-laying operation in Highley where Lesley lived, there had also been sewer and pipe-laying operations going on where each of the three sub-postmasters were killed. Police believed the killer was a pipe-layer or site manager and they were hell bent on finding the men known to have worked at the sites where the crimes took place. As police searched the Bathpool Park tunnels, more secrets were revealed and a maniac's double life 60ft below ground was beginning to surface. They found a sleeping bag, binoculars, a torch and a cassette recorder, while divers found more significant clues in a 50ft stretch of underground canal close by. Lesley's slippers were recovered from the scene – and not the car as the police had earlier stated – and Commander Morrison gave a press conference on 12th March 1975 which brought about a new mood of optimism. They knew that the Panther left Lesley tied up with wire while he went shopping for equipment in Boots, Woolworths and Halfords. Meanwhile, on 14th March 1975, the same day that Lesley's funeral was held at the parish church in Highley, a man was held for questioning by police.

He was detained after teams of armed police swooped on a house at Halesowen, Worcestershire. He was taken to Dudley police station and questioned by Bob Booth, head of West Mercia CID. By

22nd March, professional criminals had joined forces with the police in the hunt for the Panther. A special telephone information service at the murder-hunt headquarters had more than 100 calls from underworld tipsters. A senior officer said: "The criminal fraternity are using this service to name men they have served with in prison who they think could be the man we are seeking. It is very rare for us to get this kind of help and we are following up all the information." In addition, the firm who built the sewer system where Lesley's body was found made an appeal in its company magazine for information from anyone who may have known the killer – believed to have been a construction worker.

By the following month, police were using a computer known as the "brain", a machine able to pinpoint vehicles stolen anywhere in the country in under a minute. The Panther had been known to steal cars and it was believed that he was on his third stolen vehicle. "The computer could be a shortcut to finding it", said police, and, on 9th April, the hunt for the killer moved to Nottingham when police discovered that false registration numbers used by the Panther were copied from two cars regularly parked in the city. More than 1,000 people had rung the murder headquarters with information after a televised reconstruction of the Panther's movements by actor David Miller, and the police were confident that they had the killer's identity among the 10,000 names already given to murder squad detectives as suspects. However, by November 1975, the investigation still hadn't apprehended the killer. A new approach was taken by police as they began a systematic new search, which it was hoped would trap the murderer through his handwriting. The task was to sift through nearly 400,000 application forms for driving licences received by Staffordshire motor taxation office since 1970. Twelve handwriting experts from the murder hunt headquarters were tasked with the painstaking work.

In December 1975, Donald Neilson (formerly Donald Nappey), met the fury of a hostile crowd as he arrived at court, accused of being the Black Panther, responsible for the deaths of four innocent victims. Two hundred jeering, shouting people pressed forward as the police car carrying the accused arrived at the magistrates' court in Newcastle-under-Lyme, Staffordshire. Dozens of extra police were on duty to keep back the crowd as 39-year-old Neilson, his head covered by a blanket, was led into court. When Neilson, the father of a teenage girl, was asked if he had anything to say, he replied in a strong clear voice: "Not guilty, sir." The joiner from Bradford was then remanded in custody. The hearing of committal proceedings was to be held in Kidsgrove in late March 1976. By this time, Neilson had already made 17 appearances in court charged with the murder of Lesley, the murders of the three sub-postmasters, three attempted murders, kidnapping and demanding money with menaces. In June that year, he appeared at Oxford Crown Court for the charges brought against him.

Neilson sobbed in court and sat with his head hidden in his hands as the court heard Lesley Whittle's voice on tape. He had admitted to kidnapping the heiress on 14th June 1976, but denied her murder. In the taped message played to a packed courtroom,

Lesley first gave details of Neilson's £50,000 ransom instructions. Then she added this message to her mother: "There is no need to worry, mum. I am OK. I got a bit wet but I am dry now." The court heard that throughout her ordeal, Lesley had remained naked. A sleeping bag had been her only cover. It was also revealed that Neilson had coolly and meticulously planned Lesley's kidnap for three years. The prosecution argued that Neilson killed Lesley when his plans went wrong. He had selected the Whittle family as a blackmail target in 1972 when he read reports about disputes over Lesley's father's will. Neilson, who had probably been responsible for around 400 house burglaries before he turned to violent crime and murder, had carefully calculated all his plans for the kidnapping. The court heard how during two days of interviews he told police: "I estimated £50,000 would be sufficient for me to finish with crime. I reckoned the mother would immediately pay a ransom of this amount for the son, or, alternatively, the son, for the mother." He had never intended to make Lesley Whittle his victim. He broke into the Whittle home through a back door. "I went upstairs. I went into the first bedroom on the right. There was someone in bed. I woke the person and said: 'Don't make any noise. I want money.' The person replied: 'It's in the bathroom.' I said: 'You show me.' A girl got out of bed. She was naked. I said: 'Put on some clothes.'" In the statement he describes how he pushed the girl downstairs and carried her to his car. He then described returning to the house and leaving the ransom demand before driving to Bathpool Park and hiding Lesley 60ft underground. Neilson strenuously denied pushing Lesley off the ledge in the shaft and said that she fell and there was nothing he could do to save her. He described how, "Her eyes flickered and stopped. It is fair to say I panicked."

Neilson's "trail of blood" had ended when two patrolling policemen thought he was acting suspiciously and tried to question him. He had got into the patrol car and threatened the officers with a shotgun. After some stunt driving by one of the officers, Neilson was eventually overpowered by the policemen and two men at a fish-and-chip shop in Rainworth.

He was convicted of all four murders and was described by the judge as: "A killer without mercy." He was jailed for the rest of his life on 21ʰ July 1976. The judge ordered that a life sentence "must mean life". Neilson showed no emotion as he was sentenced at Oxford Crown Court. It had taken the jury five hours to find him guilty.

He was also given a life sentence for causing grievous bodily harm to Mrs Peggy Grayland and 21 years for kidnapping Lesley Whittle, 10 years for demanding a £50,000 ransom, 10 years on each of two burglary charges and 10 years for possessing a firearm with intent to endanger life. For five years, this man, operating as the Black Panther, had struck fear into every sub-post office in the country. He saw himself as a man who could outwit the police again and again. After becoming a successful small-time burglar, Neilson had moved into the big league after stealing two shotguns from a house in Dewsbury, Yorkshire. He took to his new role as an armed robber with ease. Neilson, with his birthname, Nappey, had been bullied and abused both as a child and as a soldier in the army for 20 years. He had become sullen and morose and was the only boy from his primary school not to go to grammar school. His mother died when he was 11 and he became more and more withdrawn. He had married a local girl, Irene Tate, at the age of 18 but was unpopular with his in-laws. He changed the family surname to Neilson after his daughter was born so that she wouldn't suffer the same fate with bullying once she was old enough for school. For family holidays he would take his wife and daughter to the most remote places in the country he could find and make them dress in battle gear. They were then ordered to find him on lonely moors as part of "operational manoeuvres". He ran his home with a frightening show of military discipline. He would make his daughter, Kathryn, undergo army-style "jankers" if she misbehaved, with such punishments as moving piles of bricks from one side of the yard to the other. When he discovered that Kathryn, aged 16, had drunk beer in a pub, he imprisoned her in her bedroom for a fortnight on a diet of toast. He also turned his wife, Irene, into a criminal by using fear as a weapon to make her obey him. This would eventually lead him to kidnap, terror and murder.

In 2008, Donald Neilson applied to the High Court for a minimum term to be set to give him a chance of parole. However, Mr Justice Teare ruled that his "whole life" tariff must remain. Neilson died in prison in December 2011 following two years of motor neurone disease, the muscle-wasting illness. He was aged 75. Stuart Mackenzie, one of the "hero" police officers who helped bring Neilson's reign of terror to an end, described the former Black

Panther as "pure evil" and said: "Prison was too good for him. I'm a great believer in an eye for an eye and anyone who takes a life doesn't deserve to walk God's earth." The retired officer added: "Neilson has had a life of luxury in jail while the families of his victims have had to work for a living. It really grieves me that their lives have been ruined while he was being looked after, fed and clothed. He never showed any remorse. I just hope his death has brought some closure for the families of the people he killed."

Ben Needham

(1991)

In July 1991, 21-month-old Ben Needham was snatched on the Greek island of Kos. Police feared in early August that the toddler may have been taken in order to be sold to a childless couple. Hundreds of homes on the Greek isle were searched after the child went missing. Police chief Stefos Dionysopoulos said he had picked up all kinds of reports through interviews with locals, stating: "We are now investigating every possibility including that of a financial transaction over the child." Fears grew that Ben had been kidnapped after a massive search of a forest near the spot where he disappeared drew a blank. The boy went missing from outside a house being modernized by the parents of his 20-year-old mother, Kerry, who was working at a nearby hotel. Ben's father, Simon Ward, 21, had left Kos three days before Ben vanished, amid reports of a row with Kerry. But he returned to the island to join the hunt for his son. Looking pale and tearful before leaving Newcastle airport with brothers Paul and Chris, he vowed to do all he could to find Ben. He angrily dismissed the suggestion that the child could have been kidnapped for sale. "I have never heard anything so ridiculous as to suggest my son has been sold like some pet animal", he said. "If the police over there are saying that, I find it incredible." Simon, a decorator, pledged to fight "malicious gossip" that he had snatched Ben, adding: "I have got to believe he is safe and well." He went on to describe how he had heard all sorts of rumours about the disappearance of his son, but stated: "I won't know the truth until I get there." Extra security was given to the island's ports to block any attempt to smuggle Ben out. The police had also taken formal statements from Kerry, her parents and her 17-year-old brother, Stephen.

Heartbroken, Kerry Needham returned to Britain alone, six weeks after her baby son went missing. Police and troops had searched Kos but had found no trace of the blond-haired child. Simon also returned home to Sheffield after police abandoned their search.

More than a year after Ben went missing, Kerry held up a computer-generated picture of how her son would look in the hope that it might spark a lead in the case into his disappearance. Police created the new likeness of Ben by "aging" a photo taken just before he vanished in Greece. The picture was to be featured on posters distributed to police stations throughout Greece, and on leaflets handed to British holidaymakers. The words to accompany the picture read: "Ben was last seen in July 1991 on the island of Kos, where his family were rebuilding a remote farmhouse." Police believed he could have been in the hands of travellers in the Greek islands. Kerry, who lived in Sheffield with Simon Ward said: "I often try to picture how he looks now. There's not a minute goes by that I'm not thinking of him." Kerry begged anyone going to Greece to take a camera. "If you see a boy like my Ben, please, please take a photo of him and give it to the police as soon as you can." She added: "I'm convinced Ben is still alive. He must be speaking

Greek by now. I sometimes wonder what he'll be like when I get him back." She also spoke of how the police and the public were keeping their hopes "alive".

Later that same month, on 22nd September, Kerry was described in the newspapers as a "shattered kidnap mum" after she raced 2,000 miles to see a blond-haired child who might have been her son. She wept bitter tears of disappointment as soon as she laid eyes on the child. It wasn't Ben. As the confused little boy eyed her warily, Kerry tenderly drew him into her arms and sobbed: "I wish you were Ben. Why couldn't you be him?" The poignant meeting took place in a Corfu bar after an amazing series of coincidences led to 17 separate sightings by British tourists, following the release of the new "aged" pictures of Ben. Kerry had also made a desperate appeal in the *Mirror* asking readers to look out for her child. She hardly dared to believe it would do any good, but the reports began to flood in: "fair-haired, blue-eyed toddler about the right age, always in the company of a Greek couple much too old to be his natural parents". Six of them originated from the same bar on Corfu, 500 miles from the island of Kos where Ben vanished. Even the police in Sheffield were convinced. "We have never had a lead as good as this", said Sergeant Bert Norburn, the man co-ordinating the British hunt. "I feel this has to be Ben Needham." The British police could not work in Greece, so the *Mirror* agreed to help in the secret operation to investigate the sightings. As the newspaper flew Kerry and her mother Christine to Corfu, they finally dared to hope.

They made straight for Yani's – the tourist bar where the child had been sighted – in the resort of Kassiopi. For an hour the two women sat in silent prayer, nervously scanning the other customers. Their anxious faces were hidden behind dark glasses in case the people holding "Ben" should recognize them. "Suddenly a blond boy of about three darted through the door… and the precious hope in Kerry's heart died", wrote Jim Oldfield in the *Mirror*. They had travelled 2,000 miles only to be disappointed by cruel coincidence, for little Panos, the child who had sparked the excitement, was born in Greece to British parents. He was the right age and did bear a strong resemblance to Ben. But he had been given by his unmarried mum to a childless couple from Corfu, probably the only such adoption ever to take place in the Greek islands. When the child's father heard Kerry's story he was full of sympathy and concern. The 63-year-old property developer, who didn't want to be named, was one of Corfu's wealthiest men. Having given up hope of ever becoming parents, he and his wife learned of a young British girl living on the island who was putting her baby up for adoption. He said: "We love him so much. If anyone took Panos I don't know what we would do. We feel so very sorry for this girl, coming all this way for nothing." At first, Kerry could only collapse in her mother's arms but she then began to realize she had found a strange kind of relief amid the disappointment that had "knocked her sideways" when she first saw Panos. Until then, she had been tortured by fears that she might not recognize her son if she should see him. "He must have changed so much", she said. "All this time I have been riddled with guilt wondering if I would know his face, but as soon as I saw that little boy, I knew it wasn't Ben. And, I know now that I will recognize him... however long it takes." She explained that she now knew that there was something between a mother and her baby "that even time cannot take away". However, meeting Panos had brought Kerry back to her original fears and suspicions that Ben was abducted by one of the bands of "gypsies" roaming the Greek islands, although she was certain that "when the time comes, I will know him".

When Ben went missing on 24th July 1991, he had been playing outside the farmhouse his grandparents were renovating. When the police failed to uncover a single clue, they then pulled the Needham family in for days of relentless questioning. When they finally accepted that the family were innocent of any part in Ben's disappearance, the trail had gone cold. By 1992, despite hundreds of sightings – mainly from British tourists – the police were no closer to finding him. Christine Needham described it as "like a jigsaw, but after all this time, we still don't have any of the pieces".

Five months later, in January 1993, a massive new search was launched by the Greek Army to find the 3-year-old child. British Prime Minister John Major was backing Kerry Needham's pressure on the Greek authorities to order a new search of the islands. Two months later, having suffered the enormous pressure and strain of losing their child, Kerry and Simon broke up. As Simon moved out of the couple's flat in Sheffield, Kerry blamed the rift on the pressure of Ben's disappearance. She admitted that she felt the break-up was her fault because she was unable to put Ben out of her mind. She said: "I think about Ben 24 hours a day and that's all I ever want to talk about." Simon had tried, and had wanted for the couple to lead a normal life, but Kerry was struggling with the idea. She hoped that she and Simon would remain friends so that they could both be there when Ben came home.

There was more heartache for the family when a suspicious tourist, John Cookson, grabbed a hair from the head of a blond child called Savvas who he spotted on the Greek island of Rhodes in 1998. He was convinced that the child was Ben and wanted to bring the hair back for DNA testing. However, the 53-year-old father of the boy, Nico Skyllarakis said: "Our hearts go out to Ben's family but we haven't stolen their child." Nico admitted that he couldn't produce a birth certificate for his son, but his passport did give the boy's date of birth as 28th August 1991 – one month after Ben disappeared. So convinced was John Cookson that the 7-year-old boy was Ben that he even produced a video of the child.

In May 2003, Ben's parents set up a website in the hope that their son might find it. Kerry was convinced that Ben was still alive. She had repeatedly returned to Kos to follow-up false sightings of him there, as well as elsewhere in the world. She stated in 2003: "We found out there are a lot of child-selling agencies over there. I'm very hopeful the website will help us find him. I think about him every day and wonder where he is and what sort of life he is leading." The site included the last photo of Ben and a computer image of how he might have looked at the age of 13. Private investigator Ian

Crosby, who set up the site, also believes that Ben was abducted and sold. He said: "The site opens up the search and means that there is every chance Ben himself could come across it." It was to be the first in a series of websites designed to help find Ben and to keep his story alive. Thoughts that he'd been kidnapped were still at the forefront of peoples' minds.

In May 2007, Kerry Needham urged the parents of missing Madeleine McCann to "hold on". She revealed that she still hadn't given up hope that she would be reunited with Ben 16 years after he went missing. She said of the McCanns: "All they can do is rely on the police and other support." Kerry still hoped that "one day her boy will walk through the door". She said: "All I have left is my mother's instinct which says 'hold on'. I am waiting for Ben to find me because I believe one day he will." By 2007 Kerry had got married and became known as Mrs Grist, but she revealed how her ordeal has never ended. In 2007, newspapers reported how: "To this day she keeps a room empty in readiness for his return." The distress felt by Kate and Gerry McCann brought back Kerry's own memories of loss and helplessness. Her own experience had been very different, however. For Kerry there had been no support from the British Embassy and there were no trauma counsellors, criminal behaviour experts, lawyers, or PR people to help her. No money was ever raised in the search for her son. To pay for her fare home, she had been forced to sell Ben's toys, although she kept his teddies. A further image of Ben as he would have looked on his 18th birthday was released on 10th October 2007. Heartbroken

Kerry prayed it would reunite her with her missing child. Then in December 2011, the High Court ruled that British police could use a blood sample taken from Ben before he was kidnapped to match his DNA with any samples provided by the Greek authorities. After the court ruling, Kerry said: "It's a huge breakthrough. It's been a long process over about six or seven months, but the end result is obviously amazing." She continued: "I think this is the first time any mother would wish that their child has committed an offence in whichever country that he's in." Ben had been given a Guthrie heel-prick blood test when he was born in Boston Hospital, Lincolnshire on 29th October 1989. The DNA has been stored by the NHS ever since, while police confirmed that it could be matched with any other profiles.

Hollywood actor Tom Cruise joined the hunt for Ben in January 2012 after a 24-hour mega-tweet, entitled "tweet4Ben". Cruise spread the word among his 2.4 million Twitter followers – and caused a massive surge of supportive messages on the social network site. Tom Arnold and Kym Marsh were also touched by the campaign and likewise informed all their own fans. Kerry could only sit and watch as one after another of the messages – all people wanting to help in the search for Ben – came in, including from many celebrities. "I just couldn't believe it", said Kerry. "It shows that people, whoever they are, care." Meanwhile, the Greek authorities had officially reopened the case and UK police had travelled to Kos to liaise with their counterparts. Kerry said: "His 22nd birthday was three months ago. I think about him every day. I will never give up." Then in May 2012, Greek investigators launched a new search for Ben by digging up tons of earth piled yards from the farmhouse where the toddler disappeared. Their theory suggested that Ben might have been buried by accident after wandering to the nearby site. The Greeks wanted British police to provide 3D ground scanners capable of detecting human bones buried beneath rubble, while a source close to the investigation said specialist officers sent from Athens believed a full excavation should be carried out. "They would like access to the sophisticated equipment and forensic expertise which British police have at their disposal", said the source. The *Mirror* tracked down JCB driver Konstantinos Barkas, who confirmed he had excavated earth for a new property to be built 50 yards away, while Kerry said: "For the first time I believe the police want to find my son." She was speaking of her new hope 21 years after her son vanished. And JCB driver Mr Barkas, when asked if he was working on the site during the crucial first three hours after Ben went missing, said, 'Yes, I was the man with the JCB that day." He stated: "Loads of earth was being taken to clear the ground for the new house down the road. Cutting that much ground from the hill was a big job. I think people were misled in thinking the child was abducted. Could there have been an accident? I don't think so but no one really knows what happened." He continued: "The little boy was 2 years old and the thorns in that field were as high as my waist. I remember I was still there when Kerry's brother Stephen, Ben's uncle, came back late in the afternoon and told me the boy was missing. I will never forget that."

The sensational development raised serious questions about whether Ben could have died in such appalling circumstances. As well as the suspicion that he was accidentally buried after wandering off, other theories suggested (by sources of the *Mirror*) included him being a victim of a fatal accident before the culprit hid him in a shallow grave, knowing it would be further covered by tons of earth. There were also suggestions that the child could have been murdered and buried at the site, which was on the east of the island.

Kerry's parents had emigrated to Kos, taking their sons Stephen and Daniel with them to the farmhouse owned by their Greek friend, Michaelis Kypreos, who had enlisted Eddie Needham for the renovation work. Christine and Eddie recall eating lunch outside with Michaelis to escape the searing heat. At about 2.30pm, Christine realized that Ben had gone quiet while playing outdoors and searched for him on the surrounding land. At least three hours passed before the frantic grandparents contacted police to report the child missing. Greek detectives were increasingly convinced (and still are) that the most likely explanation was that Ben died on the day he vanished. "This idea is a lot more plausible than Ben being abducted", said a Greek source. "Going back 20 years, there were only two or three families up there", continued the source. "There would be no reason for anyone else to go up there. A stranger would have needed to be watching the house beforehand, and then would have snatched him in broad daylight before secreting him off the island by boat or plane. Such an operation would have required massive organization." What the Greek source then said is: "What cops do know for sure is that the dumper truck was driving up and down the track next to the house. This carried on in the days and weeks after Ben had been reported missing." On the day he went missing, a handful of officers arrived in the dark at the house in Iraklis, above Kos Town, but the nearby mound was never the focus of a proper search. The site was thick with rubble and rubbish from the building work. Today, this mound forms a steep bank covered by 2ft of grass and weeds, grown over soil and lumps of concrete.

The officers sent to Kos to head up the new team in 2011 thought Ben could have been covered over with soil and stones when the truck driver emptied a load of earth. Detective Chief Inspector Matt Fenwick, of South Yorkshire Police, visited the island in 2011 with a colleague when the case was reopened. According to *Daily Mirror* sources, they were told about the burial theory along with other lines of inquiry. The South Yorkshire police confirmed that they were "undertaking a review" of the Greek police's findings. However, Kerry believes that Ben was snatched by someone driving a white car along the lane at the time. The car sighting was reported to Kos police by the four builders working on the new house, including Mr Barkas. Eddie Needham is also still clinging to the hope that his grandson is still alive. Speaking in October 2012 he said: "I can't believe Ben died out there as we were looking. Even the police at the time believed he was alive. They told us his body would have been found by a goat herder, or God forbid, by wild animals. But if Ben was deliberately placed under rubble and earth then a new excavation is worth it." He concludes though: "But why has it taken them 20 years?" Kerry also revealed that in the hours after Ben went missing only a handful of blundering officers arrived to look for him, while one neighbour of the family in Kos claimed that the Greek police's search for the little boy was simply not thorough enough. Kerry also told journalists that in the vital hours after Ben's disappearance the officers who arrived didn't even bring torches, despite the fact it was dark. Fields surrounding the house where he was last seen were not sealed and evidence may have been missed. Stating that the police blamed her family for Ben's disappearance, she told how her mother and two police officers had come to find her as she was finishing work at 9.50pm. Christine Needham was naturally hysterical by this time and could hardly get the words "I can't find Ben" out of her mouth. Speaking to the *Daily Mirror* in May 2012 she said: "If the police want to dig up this mound it's up to them, but I think it would be a waste of time and money. I don't want to think about it. I think it's impossible that he was buried there. The searches that my mum and dad did of the area convince me he's not dead. To my mind that part of the investigation, searching around the house, was the only part that was properly done." Kerry's belief that Ben is still alive hardly wavers. Kerry has suffered hundreds of false alarms and has been plagued by psychics. "Losing a child sends you to the brink of insanity. I have been there many times. You're trying to come to terms with something that only happens in films and nightmares", she said. On her last visit to Kos, Kerry was told by the public prosecutor: "With my heart I want to find your son." This gave her a massive sense of relief after all the years she'd waited to be taken seriously by the Greek authorities. Kerry felt that as a young mother she had not been viewed in quite the same way that she was in early 2012 – a 40-year-old woman, running her own business, who had never given up looking for her son. She also said how having South Yorkshire police "at the end of a phone" had changed her life. Speaking of her years of pain, Kerry said: "I dream I've found him. Then I wake and the hurt really hits again." The energy she still devotes to finding her son is undiminished, despite her long hours of work.

In July 2012, the police travelled to Kos to search for Ben. The cold case team, led by Detective Inspector Matt Fenwick, held further discussions with Greek colleagues as part of the ongoing review. In October 2012, it was revealed that the Home Office had given permission for British police to dig up the land on Kos, alongside the Greek authorities. Kerry attended, supported by a family liaison officer, while a dog trained to search for human remains was used at the site. Having spent two decades believing that her son just could not be buried at the site and was, in fact, alive and well somewhere in the world, Kerry broke down on 18th October 2012 and admitted that, for the first time, she was beginning to have "horrifying doubts". The new search had given her doubts for the first time in more than 20 years. But, she also said that: "If they find Ben's body, I'm finished. I don't want to hear they have found my son's bones. I want to hear that he is alive, well and happy. I want them to do this search and then rule it out. Then we can all move on and concentrate on finding my son." The police were interested in anything that might identify the movements of Ben, any item of clothing, any toys, anything Ben may have been playing with. They had already carried out regressive interviews with all the Needham family about the land and all the circumstances at the time of the little boy's disappearance. The police had carried out a considerable amount of background work before they visited Kos and began their new search. The police did find bits of old toys that Ben might have been playing with as excavation experts used a JCB digger to cut away massive chunks of the mound. They also swept the area with a metal detector and found chunks of toys that could have been the Dinky cars Ben had with him when he vanished. Supported by her mum Christine, Kerry fought back tears as she thanked the Greek people for their help and then appealed to the world to keep looking for her son. She also thanked the UK specialist search teams personally and faced her fears by returning to the search site close to the farmhouse where Ben went missing. On 25th October 2012, Kerry Needham (by now she was separated from her husband), flew out of Kos with renewed hope that Ben would still be found alive. Police digging where it was suggested he could have accidentally been buried had found no trace of the missing child. They may not have found Ben, but it put the spotlight back on the case and gave new hope to the mother who has never given up looking for her son. One day – as she still believes – they will be reunited.

Sarah Payne

(2000)

Devastated Sara Payne clutched the hand of her husband Michael at a news conference on 3rd July 2000 where she begged for the return of their missing daughter, Sarah. The mum of the lost 8-year-old sobbed: "Who has got our 'little princess'?" Sara Payne begged for news amid increasing fears for the youngster's safety. Sara, 31, said: "She is our life. We need her home now, today." Sarah vanished within just 150 yards of her grandparents' home in West Sussex. Police hunting two suspect vehicles seen in the area said: "We are very, very worried." Sarah had been playing in a field behind her grandparents' home with her brothers Lee, 13, Luke, 11, and her sister, Charlotte, aged 6. Fed up with the game of dinosaurs, she said she wanted to go home and wandered towards the lane that would take her 150 yards to safety. She was followed by her brother Lee, but when he arrived at their grandparents' home, Sarah was nowhere to be seen. Sara Payne told the press conference that Sarah's brothers and sister were not coping well without her. She said: "We're a strong family and we don't survive well apart... Our family name for Sarah is our little princess, and that's just what she is. She's a soft, gentle little girl. She hasn't got a horrible bone in her body." By 3rd July, there were increasing fears that Sarah had been abducted. Police wanted to trace a white Transit-style van with no rear windows and a grey Mondeo seen in the area.

Sarah vanished at about 7pm after playing in the cornfield with her siblings. Sara Payne said: "They play a lot where they were, and Sarah knew exactly how to get home from there. She's quite a nervous girl. She wouldn't wander off on her own because she's not like that." At her side, 31-year-old Michael Payne trembled uncontrollably. He was so distraught he could not speak. Lee Payne told police that he'd seen the Mondeo and the van drive past near Sarah's route home. He had been just two minutes behind his sister. Leading the hunt for Sarah was Detective Superintendent Alan Ladley, who told the news conference at Littlehampton: "We are very, very concerned. Sarah has been missing for two nights and we are obviously considering the possibility she was pushed into a van or car." He was confident that the 8-year-old child would have already been found had she been close by where she went missing. "We appeal to the drivers of the van and Mondeo to come forward", he said.

By 3rd July 2000, 150 officers were involved in the search. A squad of 50 detectives were ordered to interview every known paedophile in the area. West Sussex police were also searching for a serial sex attacker who had indecently assaulted a girl of 12 and raped a woman in 14 suspected attacks. Police said that there was no obvious link with Sarah's disappearance, but that they were keeping an open mind. Meanwhile, underwater search teams were brought in and a sniffer dog was given a piece of Sarah's clothing to catch her scent. The dog was taken by his handler into the cornfield where the child was last seen. After 20 minutes hunting through the corn, he bounded out of the field and pulled his handler back towards the grandparents' house. The area was covered with fast-growing crops, as well as dense brambles and nettles. The team was also joined by a police helicopter and an RAF Meteor flying low over the village, using infra-red equipment. Members of the public and military police from Chichester scoured fields and woods. A description of Sarah and the clothing she was wearing was given to the public in the hope that she would be found in a shed or outbuilding. But as the third night of searching approached, officers privately feared the youngster may not have been alive at this point. One said: "In the absence of any reported sighting we have to face the possibility that she was grabbed by someone and is either being held captive, or has suffered an even worse fate."

By 11th July 2000, police had an e-fit of a suspect and begged the public to help them track him down. The man, about 30 and 6ft tall, was described as white, solidly built, with distinctive crinkly sandy hair, a strong jaw and wide nose. He was wearing washed-out black jeans, a dark grey bomber jacket and plum shirt. He was seen with a sobbing girl, resembling Sarah, at a motorway service area nine hours after the little girl vanished 250 miles away. Despite police appeals, the man hadn't come forward to eliminate himself from inquiries. DS Alan Ladley said: "Clearly, if this girl was Sarah it's a vital line of inquiry and we'll pursue it to the very end." The distressed girl was seen by a woman at 5am in a ladies toilet at Knutsford Services on the northbound M6 in Cheshire on Sunday 2nd July. She gave her name as Sarah and spoke in a southern accent. Police revealed that the woman comforted the child and "tidied her up". The youngster left the toilets and was joined by the suspect who was waiting nearby. The woman witness asked him: "Is she with you?" He replied "Yes", in a neutral accent. The pair then left hand-in-hand, making the woman believe nothing was amiss.

It was already known that the girl seen at the motorway services bore a startling resemblance to Sarah – she looked the same age and height, had blonde hair of the same length and she was wearing a thin blue short-sleeved dress and dark, possibly black shoes. Sarah had vanished wearing black shoes and a blue sports dress. The woman witness was said to be "upset" that she hadn't done more to help the girl, but at the time it wasn't public knowledge that Sarah had gone missing. After the e-fit was published, calls poured in from all over Britain and Europe, including Spain, Greece and Germany. Earlier the same day, police in South Wales scrambled a helicopter after a girl fitting Sarah's description was seen with a man near the village of Cilfynydd, but the search proved negative.

In an exclusive interview with *Daily Mirror* journalist Sue Carroll, Sara and Michael Payne told how they refused to lose hope for their daughter's safe return. On 14th July 2000 they told Sue Carroll of their aching torment. It had been two weeks since their young daughter had gone missing. Sara Payne said: "We're not hopeful, we're certain. Call it gut instinct. I just know one day she'll come bounding through our door." In the harrowing interview, Michael revealed that each morning he had an imaginary conversation with his daughter, he said: "It's along the lines of, 'Hello sweetheart. I love you and I miss you.' It's so quiet without her." Sara revealed that the first thing she did every morning after a few hours of fitful sleep is say "Good morning" and kiss her favourite picture of her daughter. The couple also told how they had wept bitter tears with their other children while the police hunt continued. The police had turned to the Internet in the search for the missing child and revealed that they were examining a suspect white van.

Sue Carroll reports:

"Like everyone else in Britain I have seen the Paynes' very public anguish being played out to the nation at televised press conferences, and my heart has gone out to them. But sitting next to the couple clinging to one another and seeing for myself their extraordinary courage, calmness and implacable belief that some day soon their little girl will come through the door, was a humbling experience."

She writes: "Gaunt and utterly exhausted, puffing on the cigarettes they have sworn to quit when Sarah comes home, Sara and Michael are wired on the adrenaline of sheer desperation." Understandably, the family had remained in West Sussex where the massive police hunt was based, rather than returning home to Surrey. "We can't go home without her", said her mother.

The couple, who had been married for 10 years, clearly had a formidable bond (although they were to split in 2003 due to the pressure of losing Sarah). Both felt that they had lost their power as parents when Sarah was taken, and continuing with the press conferences was their way of staying connected to their daughter.

It was their own way of expressing that Sarah was still theirs and always would be. Meanwhile, switching the hunt to the Internet, police urged computer owners to print her picture from a website and stick the poster in their window or in the street. They hoped that the colour photo would strike home with someone who might have seen her. The police launched their plea as they grew more and more fearful that Sarah had been murdered.

By this time (July 2000), officers had received 17,500 calls about the search, but were still no nearer finding Sarah. DS Alan Ladley confirmed: "It is frustrating for us and devastating for the family that we have not found Sarah." He said: "The history of abductions gets rewritten every time it happens, but there are a number of pieces of information that indicate she may well not be alive now." "But, until we find her," he added, "we will not give up hope. Nor will her family give up hope."

On 19th July 2000, Luke Payne stood on a flower-strewn road yards from where his little sister's body was found, took a piece of paper from his pocket and steadied himself. The 11-year-old unfolded the paper with the utmost care and made a little space for it among the bouquets and tributes already placed in memory of the 8-year-old. The message read: "You are now parted from the life of this world. I'll never forget you. I can change and learn from what's happened. I promise I will always love you, my little princess." It ended with the words: "Love you, Luke. Please help to look out for Charlotte." The whole family were numb with grief as they spent around 15 minutes unfolding letters, reading messages and sobbing. The police were now hunting for a killer, but meanwhile revealed that four campers had heard a girl screaming on the night Sarah disappeared. For more than two weeks, the family had hoped, prayed and tried to remain positive. Now they came together in grief. It had been too painful for the family to see Sarah's body, but they came to say goodbye to her on the A29, just yards from where her body was found near Pulborough in West Sussex. The optimism and determination that had so impressed the nation was replaced by an unimaginable despair.

Throughout the long search, the family had struggled to contain their emotions and put on a brave face. Now the tears flowed openly and their eyes were red raw. All day the traffic had backed up on this stretch of road. Now, it stopped out of respect for the family. After a heartbreaking news conference in which Sara and Michael Payne appealed for anyone with information to come forward, police spoke about two couples camping just three miles from where Sarah's body was found, who had heard a little girl's desperate screams on the night she disappeared. The cries shattered the rural calm of the Sussex countryside and police said it was possible that Sarah was murdered away from the spot where her body was discovered in a shallow grave. The four young people had been pitched near a stream in an isolated beauty spot on the edge of Fittleworth. A team of forensic officers would then widen their search to include that area. A senior murder squad detective said: "This could be a significant lead. We do not know precisely where Sarah was when she was killed." Alan Ladley, leading the hunt for the murderer, warned against vigilante attacks as officers searched the house of a man arrested in connection with Sarah's disappearance, who was later bailed. DS Ladley told a press conference that up to 30 local youths had hurled stones at the house in Crawley, West Sussex and shouted abuse. Officers, at this point, still did not know if Sarah was sexually abused, or how she died. They thought she may have been strangled or suffocated and they were still searching for her clothes.

By 24th July 2000, a suspect was in custody. The man, in his forties, was arrested after a police car chase and accused of stealing a car. The suspect had been staying at his father's home but was driven out by vigilantes who stoned the house. At the time of the arrest, he was living in a tent. Meanwhile, one of Sarah's black shoes had been found and was being examined for traces of forensic evidence. Despite police warnings, other vigilantes continued to stone the houses of people they suspected might have been involved in the kidnap and murder of Sarah Payne. One innocent man was targeted after vigilantes mistook him for a child abuser and the then Home Secretary, Jack Straw, slammed the News of the World for naming paedophiles after the mob attacked the innocent man's home.

On the sixteenth day after Sarah Payne vanished, Chief Constable Nigel Yeo's car nosed into Sarah's grandfather, Terry Payne's driveway. The family and Nigel Yeo had become close since Sarah's disappearance, but this was the visit they dreaded. Mr Yeo was in Terry's living room, surrounded by photographs of the little girl who had brought them together, breaking the news that the body of a young girl had been found in an overgrown field at the edge of the A29. He told the family that they should prepare themselves for the possibility that it could be Sarah. A midnight post-mortem confirmed what the Payne family already knew in their hearts – that the little girl dumped in waist-high grass and weeds was their little princess, Sarah.

Nearing the end of August, almost two months after Sarah went missing, her clothes and one shoe had still not been found. Police issued a fresh plea for information, hoping to jog the memories of anyone who had been on (or taken photos of) Kingston Gorse beach in West Sussex, just minutes away from where Sarah disappeared with her murderer. In September 2000 a witness told police that on the night Sarah vanished they were driving behind a truck that had to brake violently as a van sped out of a turning near where the little girl's body had been left. Police were seeking the lorry driver in the hope that he may have seen the face of Sarah's killer, driving the white van. Police said: "The van came out of a turning exactly where Sarah was found. His erratic driving is an indication of how nervous he would have been." The van fitted the description of the Transit-style vehicle that Lee Payne had spotted in the lane at Kingston Gorse where his sister vanished. Just three days later, Sara and Michael Payne revealed that Jack Straw had promised to change Britain's child sex laws. They were a step closer to "Sarah's Law". The couple had campaigned to strengthen Britain's paedophile legislation since their daughter was murdered. The new law would give parents the right to know if a child sex offender moved into their area. Although the couple were completely against vigilante tactics, they had supported the *News of the World*'s "name and shame" campaign and strongly believed that all parents had the right to protect their children – including information about who was living in their midst. Sarah's murder had sparked a wave of anger across the country at the lack of protection that children are given from known sex offenders. Sara and Michael were demanding legislation like Megan's Law in the US, which was introduced and so-named after a little girl was killed by a known paedophile in America. The battle for Sarah's Law was won in September 2000 when Home Office minister Paul Boateng said the government had agreed to allow public access to lists of paedophiles. The change in the law was also backed by 93,000 readers of the *Mirror*. More than 700,000 readers of the *News of the World* also backed the campaign calling for Sarah's Law. The family revealed that Jack Straw had agreed to their demands for tougher sentencing of paedophiles and more powers for the families of victims.

Meanwhile, the man arrested by police following a car chase was jailed for 22 months at the end of September for unrelated motoring offences. Builder, Roy Whiting, 41, was questioned by detectives over the killing of Sarah, but released without charge. On 27th September, he admitted one charge of dangerous driving and one of taking a vehicle without consent. The court heard how his life had been "ripped apart" when he was arrested on 2nd July 2000 in connection with Sarah's disappearance. The former mechanic stole a Vauxhall Nova because he had lost his home and needed a roof over his head. But when police spotted him he "panicked" and sped off. During the chase in the early hours of 23rd July, Whiting tried to ram two police cars and drove through 30mph zones at up to 60mph. Judge Anthony Thorpe described his driving as "lunatic" and said that the terrified police believed they could have been killed if they had not swerved to avoid the Nova. Whiting left his flat in Littlehampton, West Sussex after the 2nd July arrest and went to stay with his 80-year-old father in Crawley. He was forced to leave after vigilantes stoned the property. Whiting was disqualified from driving for three years.

In December 2000, it was thought Sarah's killer might finally be caught thanks to aerial photographs of the kidnap scene, police revealed. The images were taken shortly before the 8-year-old was snatched. Detectives, using the latest technology to enhance the pictures, hoped to trace a white Transit-style van her killer was thought to have used. By January 2001, it was thought that a length of old curtain could also help catch Sarah's killer. The distinctive curtain had a clown pattern on a blue striped background and it was thought that Sarah could have come into contact with it after she was abducted. Police were unwilling to go into details for legal reasons, but said it was vitally important to trace the curtain's origins. In early February 2001, it was revealed that Roy Whiting was to be quizzed for the third time by police over Sarah's murder. There had been a "vital breakthrough" in the hunt for the little girl's murderer and forensic scientists were believed to have recovered a tiny speck of DNA from the curtains thought to be linked to the murder. It apparently matched DNA taken from one of Sarah's baby teeth, which had been kept by her mother. It was a crucial development for police in the protracted search for Sarah's killer. By this time, a white Transit-style van had been traced and seized by detectives. Divorced father of one, Whiting, was one of a number of men arrested soon after Sarah disappeared. He was released on police bail after being questioned, but was re-arrested on 31st July when he was again freed by murder detectives. However, on 6th February 2001, Roy Whiting was charged with the kidnap and murder of 8-year-old Sarah. The 42-year-old was arrested at 9.17am in Kent and driven to Bognor Regis police station for questioning. He was charged at 3.20pm with the murder of Sarah Payne.

Detective Superintendent Peter Kennett said: "He was also additionally charged with the kidnap of Sarah." Whiting appeared at Chichester Magistrates' Court at 10am on 7th February. Sara and Michael Payne were informed by police of the arrest and charges against Whiting. When the accused appeared in court, the police clashed with an angry mob throwing missiles. The 200-strong crowd then gave chase when the vehicle carrying Whiting drove away from the building. More than 40 officers formed a cordon to hold the furious demonstrators back. Whiting had stood in court with his arms crossed throughout the 38-minute hearing and spoke only to confirm his name and date of birth. He was remanded in custody until his appearance at Lewis Crown Court on 19th February 2001.

On the actual day, in Court No. 3, Sara Payne sat in dignified silence within arm's length of the man accused of the kidnap and murder of her daughter. She never once flinched from her determined stare as she sat in the public gallery clutching the hand of her husband Michael. Unlike the baying mob at Whiting's earlier court appearance, Sara uttered no sound. Whiting was remanded until 18th May. In court, the jury heard on 14th November 2001 how the murderer of schoolgirl Sarah grinned and waved at her brother as he drove the little girl away to her death. Sarah had started to make her way out of the field and when she got halfway towards a gap in the hedge, Luke had caught up with her and told her to wait. He then went back to Lee and Charlotte in the field but Sarah decided to go on towards the gap. Lee saw this and ran diagonally across the field towards her, but when he was halfway across, Sarah had reached the gap. She went through it and that was the last any of her family saw of her. Prosecuting QC, Timothy Langdale, told the jury that as Lee was crossing the field he saw a white van being driven along the lane beside the cornfield. As Lee reached the gap in the hedge and began to walk towards his grandparents' home, he saw a white van pulling out of an adjoining lane "as if in a hurry, with its wheels spinning", said Mr Langdale. The van then drove back the way it had come and Lee noticed that the van had no windows at the back or sides. The child saw the driver, albeit for a short space of time, and as the van passed Lee, the driver grinned at him and gave a wave with his hand. Mr Langdale told the jury: "It is the Crown's case that the driver was the defendant, Roy Whiting, and it is the Crown's case that Sarah was already in that van having been picked up, snatched up, in the lane." He added: "There is compelling evidence that points to Roy Whiting and Roy Whiting alone, as the man responsible for kidnapping this child and killing her." Mr Langdale asked the jury to be "cool" and "dispassionate" about "this horrific crime" and described to them how when Sarah's body was found it had been mutilated by animals. She had been discovered two weeks after her disappearance by farm labourer Luke Coleman on 17th July 2000. The prosecuting QC also stated that despite the lack of firm conclusion from the post-mortem report, the Crown believed that Sarah was the victim of a "sexually motivated homicide". Evidence of Sarah's presence in Whiting's van was found in the front of the vehicle, although not the back. Despite all this, disaster struck for the Crown and Sarah's family on 15th November when the trial collapsed due to a "procedural irregularity" and a second trial was ordered with a new jury. Fibres from Whiting's shirt had been found on the Velcro strap of Sarah's shoe – the only piece of clothing ever recovered, while the jury were told on 16th November that a single blonde hair from the small victim would nail her killer. The hair was found on a red sweatshirt, discovered in a white van owned by Whiting. Speaking to a new jury, Langdale said that the blonde hair – one of 24 found on Whiting's sweatshirt – was: "perhaps the most significant item in this case". He continued: "One hair found on the red sweatshirt gave a full DNA profile matching Sarah." He also confirmed that a ball of Sarah's hair mixed with soil and vegetation was left behind when her body was moved from the shallow grave. It contained 200 fibres of material – two of which matched the red sweatshirt found in Whiting's van. A blue fibre found in the hair matched a fibre in the sweatshirt. In addition, Sarah's body was found in a bag containing 400 fibres of material, one of which matched the driver's seat cover of the van. Another matched the socks found in the van while other fibres taken from a silver-coloured coat, which Sarah used to wear, matched blue fibres found in the right front pocket of Whiting's jeans. In a dramatic ending to his opening speech, Mr Langdale added:

"You can be satisfied that this wasn't a case of an accident or anything of that kind in terms of the killing of this child. The man who took her away and did whatever he did to her had two major problems. Who knows whether Sarah resisted, struggled or screamed? Who knows where she was when things happened? The other major problem that he faced was if Sarah Payne had been treated indecently, assaulted, it was by the person who abducted her and if she had lived there was a real risk she would be able to tell the tale. A real risk she would have been able to provide a description of her attacker, a description of the van and of her abductor."

He concluded: "It would appear to be unanswerable that if you found that Sarah Payne was in that van then Roy Whiting is the man who seized her, the man who killed her, and the man who disposed of her clothing and at some stage buried her body in that field."

When the pathologist gave details about Sarah's horrific death, it was too much for her anguished parents who fled court in tears. Vesna Djurovic told the court how Sarah suffered a "violent" death –

probably asphyxia – in a "sexually motivated" attack. Decomposition of the body had made it impossible to say whether Sarah suffered internal or external injuries. Dr Djurovic had to tell the jury how Sarah's hair remained attached to the underlying soil as the corpse was removed and this proved more than her family could bear. She had lost most of her hair, which came away with the roots. The body was in a "moderately advanced state of decomposition and mummification". As the pathologist gave her evidence, the jury looked shaken and stopped taking notes. Dr Djurovic said:

"In view of the circumstances of the disposal of her body, the absence of clothing or natural disease, and her previous good health, I reach the conclusion she met a violent death. In my opinion, from her appearance and the removal of clothing, her death was the result of sexually-motivated homicide."

The trial continued throughout November and, on 26th of that month, the jury were shown pictures of the inside of a van where Sarah was said to have been killed. Police removed 302 items from the white Fiat Ducato that belonged to Whiting, including a clown-patterned curtain, red sweatshirt, a bottle of baby oil, masking tape, a knife, pickaxe, shovel, spade and a rope. Sally O'Neill, defending Whiting, claimed that Sarah's hair on the red sweatshirt was "contaminated", but leading forensic scientist Raymond Chapman disputed this. Mr Chapman was backed in court by an independent forensic scientist who told the court on 1st December 2001 that he had found crucial new evidence linking Sarah with her alleged killer. He had discovered that a distinctive fibre recovered from Sarah's hair matched a fibre from the pair of socks found in Whiting's van. He told the jury his findings, using the latest technology, backing up fibre matches discovered by Home Office forensic expert Raymond Chapman.

In the witness box on 4th December, Whiting insisted that any claimed links with 8-year-old Sarah Payne were coincidence. It was coincidence, he said that he owned a long wheelbase white van with no side or rear windows, similar to one seen by Lee Payne after his sister went missing. It was coincidence that the van driver was wearing a check shirt and a similar shirt was found in his van. It was coincidence that he had driven to areas where young people might be expected to be, including a funfair. He admitted he could not remember "exactly" where he had been on the night Sarah vanished, and he also admitted to pressure-washing the inside of his van and changing the doors. He continued to maintain that he had not kidnapped and murdered the young girl. But the court heard on 6th December 2001 how the man accused of murdering Sarah was trapped as her killer by lies and overwhelming scientific evidence. Roy Whiting was accused of lying on oath, being shifty with police and not explaining DNA evidence – that showed he had only a billion-to-one chance of not being linked to the murder. Timothy Langdale, QC, prosecuting, told the jury in his closing speech that the case against Whiting was like putting together a jigsaw puzzle. He said: "There are so many pieces of the puzzle available that a picture emerges with clarity of this defendant, despite his denials, being the man who seized Sarah, killed her and buried her body."

Miss O'Neill, in her closing speech said:

"The abduction and death of Sarah Payne was a tragedy of unimaginable dimension for the family and nothing can be said or done which will lessen that tragedy. It is my intention that nothing I say will make it worse and I also hope that I don't seem to be deliberately ignoring the enormity of their loss. I'm going to ask you to stand aside from that tragedy. The one and only consideration for you in this trial is to decide whether the prosecution can make you sure that Roy Whiting is the person who abducted her and was later responsible for her death."

On 10th December the judge, Mr Justice Curtis, urged the jury to be "calm and dispassionate" when considering their verdicts. He said: "Act on all the evidence that has been presented to you... Deciding on a case like this requires courage – I know that. Do not shrink from being decisive."

The jury returned with unanimous guilty verdicts at the end of the 19-day trial. However, Whiting showed no flicker of emotion as he was sentenced for the 8-year-old's kidnap and murder and told he would never be freed. It was revealed that Whiting had been jailed for four years in 1995 for a sex attack on another schoolgirl. Mr Justice Curtis told him that he was "an absolute menace to every little girl", and added: "You are indeed an evil man. You are every parent's and every grandparent's nightmare come true." Sara Payne said, following the guilty verdicts: "Justice has been done. Sarah can rest in peace now." She added: "Please make sure that this stops happening time and time again."

Home Office minister, Beverley Hughes, said the government would use the case to learn lessons about protecting the public, while probation officials said the tragedy could have been prevented by legislation introduced a year after Whiting was released after serving two years of his four-year sentence for the 1995 conviction. He was supervised for four months, but under the Crime and Disorder Act could have been watched for 10 years. Norman Brennan, director of the Victims of Crime Trust, said that the jury should have been made aware of Whiting's previous conviction, and the Probation Officers' Union, Napo, urged the government to look again at introducing indefinite jail sentences for child sex offenders. It was possible that Whiting was responsible for a series of attempted kidnaps throughout his adult life. Police believed that many unsolved attacks on young girls were probably carried out by Whiting. After the trial, it became public that in his previous conviction Whiting had been described as a "high risk" repeat offender.

Sara Payne was awarded an MBE in 2009 for the dedicated campaigning she carried out following her daughter's kidnap and murder and was given the job of victims' representative at the Justice Ministry – a role designed to give victims a "louder voice", one that the government would listen to. However, she was later snubbed for the post of commissioner. The children's safety campaigner said that the decision not to give her the new job: "feels like a giant kick in the teeth". Further fury befell Sara Payne when Whiting's sentence was reduced from 50 to 40 years, bringing him in line with Soham killer, Ian Huntley. "All the time it was 50 years it sent a good message to the world. He should die in prison. That man is a danger to children and will be so as long as he lives and breathes", she said. Unfortunately, it seemed that many of the lessons learned over the tragic death of Sarah were never fully understood, despite the committed campaigning by the little girl's mother and others in positions able to help. Children continued to be kidnapped and brutally murdered, or never heard from again.

Madeleine McCann

(2007)

A police hunt for a missing 3-year-old was under way by 4th May 2007 after Madeleine McCann vanished from quiet Praia da Luz, a complex on Portugal's Algarve, on the night of Thursday 3rd May. Her anguished parents, Kate and Gerry McCann, had been eating at a bar 120ft away. Her scent was picked up by a police sniffer dog, but it petered out after 400 yards. The appalling news that Madeleine – also known as Maddy, particularly in the press following her disappearance – was feared kidnapped from the holiday complex came in a phone call from her distraught dad, one of Europe's top heart specialists, to his sister Trish in Scotland. Maddy had simply vanished from her cot, which was placed between 2-year-old twins, Sean and Amelie. Trish revealed that: "He was breaking his heart, saying: 'Madeleine's been abducted, she's been abducted'."

Both Kate and Gerry had been checking in on their three children every 30 minutes in the ground-floor flat while they dined with friends. But, the last time Kate went to check on her sleeping children she found the front door open, the window and the shutters in the bedroom jemmied open and Maddy gone. It was thought that someone had entered through the window of the flat and left with the small child through the front door. Maddy had disappeared from the Mark Warner Ocean club resort in the coastal village of Praia da Luz, leading to a 24-hour search by police, hundreds of villagers and British holidaymakers. They failed to find any trace of the child. The couple, from Rothley, Leicestershire, then issued a statement to say they were hopeful their daughter would be found safe and well. It read: "This is a particularly difficult time for the family and we are all comforting each other. We have received lots of support from friends, family and the public and are very grateful. All the family's focus is in assisting the authorities in securing Madeleine's return." A friend of the McCanns, one of their holiday party of nine adults and eight children, said:

"We went for dinner at 8.45pm in a restaurant near the apartments as we've done every night. A parent from each family went back to check on the children every half hour. The window shutters, which had been closed since we arrived, were open along with the window. They can be opened from the outside. The window opens on to a car park. The door to the room was shut."

All family and friends who spoke to the McCanns during these desperate early hours of their daughter's disappearance and the police investigation said that they were distraught, distressed and hysterical. They were described as desperately upset and devastated. Even in these very early hours, it seemed that the family felt the police could be doing more to find Madeleine. The McCanns' apartment was set in a self-contained complex that included villas and apartments together with supermarkets, restaurants, cafes, boutiques and bars. While there were those who spoke of jemmied shutters, Mark Warner management denied there were signs of forced entry at the flat, claiming instead that "roller shutters had been slid up and the bedroom window opened", and added that "police were keeping an open mind over whether Madeleine had managed to leave the apartment on her own". Around 60 staff and guests searched for the child until 4.30am on the night she went missing while police contacted border authorities, neighbouring Spanish officers and airports. At this point, there was a criminal investigator and around 20 officers at the abduction site, but no information, and Portuguese police said: "It's a sensitive case. It involves a child and we cannot give more information for now."

Officers sealed off the five-storey holiday block with crime-scene tape and fingerprinted the shutters and window sill outside the children's bedroom. A patio to the rear of the block, believed to be attached to the family's two-bedroom apartment, was also sealed off. By late afternoon on 5th May the hunt for the missing little girl intensified with helicopter crews, firemen and maritime search teams. A special criminal investigation team from the Polícia Judiciária was known to be travelling to the scene from Lisbon. Meanwhile, in the UK, police stood guard outside the McCann family's five-bedroom home.

Two days after Madeleine McCann went missing, her heartbroken mother wept as she begged for the kidnapped 3-year-old's safe return. Kate McCann, a GP, broke down after an emotional church service as she pleaded: "Please continue to pray for Madeleine." She was given a posy of five flowers as tears streamed down her face at the Mother's Day church service by a local child. She had been advised that the service at the Church of Our Lady of the

Light was to celebrate Mother's Day in Portugal, but the strain was etched on her face as she clutched Madeleine's toy pink cat and prayed for her daughter's safe return. Father Jose Manuel Pacheco led the prayers for Madeleine, her family and the police hunting for the kidnapped child. Pensioners, mothers and their children swarmed around the Catholic couple and kissed, hugged and shook hands with them in an extraordinary gesture of support. Many of the locals were in tears as they left the tiny church in Praia da Luz. Kate and Gerry were accompanied at the service by eight relatives, including Kate's parents, Susan and Brian Healy, who had flown to Portugal to be with their daughter and her family during what was a horrendous ordeal for them. Meanwhile, other family and friends defended the couple for leaving their three children in the apartment while they dined with their holiday companions.

In an unsettling report the newspapers claimed: "Police corruption hampers investigations into paedophiles and child traffickers in Portugal." The claims came from an international protection group, Innocence in Danger, which gave up trying to create an office in the country in 2004 due to pressure from the authorities. Homayra Sellier, the group's founder, admitted: "I stopped it because I thought I couldn't fight against a country where the people do not want to know the truth." She cited the case of Rui Pedro Mendonca, who was 11 when he disappeared from the town of Lousada in northern Portugal in March 1998. There was a sighting of him about a month later at Disneyland in Paris with a middle-aged man: "but he has never been found and may have been murdered", she said. Sellier claimed that organized criminals were operating freely in Portugal – and she believed Madeleine could have been taken by a child trafficking gang. She said:

"The fact that the girl was kidnapped from her bed shows how bad things are. Somebody who did what they did with Madeleine is beyond being a paedophile. Either he or she is totally crazy and did not even realize the risk they were taking. Or he or she was not acting on their own – somebody was waiting outside to make sure he or she could do it... Maybe now the Portuguese will wake up and realize that this is going on. Pressure can be put in this way on Portugal and the Portuguese people because many of them are scared to talk if they see something. What is in front of them is the mob and the mob goes very far up."

Launched in 1999, the Switzerland-based group Innocence in Danger had offices at the time in France, Germany and the US. It now has additional offices in the UK and Colombia.

On 7th May 2007, Kate McCann begged her daughter's captor to "let her come home". However, the detective leading the hunt said he feared "she was already dead". Chief Inspector Olegario Sousa told a press conference that he was no longer confident that the 3-year-old was still alive. Asked if he thought Maddy would be found safe and well, he replied: "I don't know." The senior officer, drafted in from Lisbon to head the case, added: "I haven't enough evidence to say. It is very difficult because I have no facts to say if the child is alive or not. We are searching for the child and until the moment she appears we do not know. We are not magicians but we are making our best efforts to locate the child." The press conference was a crushing blow for the McCann family. Just hours earlier, Kate had read out a statement begging her daughter's captor: "Please give our little girl back. Please, please don't hurt her. Please don't scare her." Still clutching the pink toy cat she had kept by her side ever since Madeleine disappeared, she choked back tears and added: "We beg you to let Madeleine come home. We need our Madeleine. Sean and Amelie need Madeleine and Madeleine needs us."

Hundreds of expats, frustrated over the police investigation, continued to search the area surrounding the resort. It emerged that detectives had an ever-growing list of suspects – including two Brits – but had not officially issued details. They had also not released details of what Madeleine was wearing – leaving it to her mother to give details of her Eeyore pyjamas. Detectives – who were still treating the case only as a missing persons inquiry – said that Interpol and Europol were working with Portuguese police, yet insisted that they were banned by law from passing any information to Madeleine's family. They had at least seven possible suspects and had searched a marina in Lagos after reports that a balding man was spotted dragging a young girl along a nearby street. Another witness said he saw a "suspicious" couple with a blonde girl close to the same marina a few hours after the child was taken. Police were also interested in a man who was spotted handing out sweets to young children in the area the week before Madeleine disappeared.

Police sources feared that Madeleine's kidnapper could have taken her from the area by boat, as officials failed to alert the maritime police of her abduction until 14 hours later. Another fear was that the kidnapper could have fled by an early morning train. The police in Portugal were slammed for 10 major blunders on 8th May when it was revealed that officers failed to seal off the holiday flat from where the small girl was kidnapped, meaning that vital clues were missed. Other tourists were allowed to stroll around the crime scene up to 24 hours later. They also delayed their search and didn't alert border guards until up to 12 hours later, so the kidnapper could have driven to Spain (an hour away). Police did not "lock down" the Mark Warner resort. Instead of amassing a huge force of officers to hunt for Madeleine, just 150 were involved in the initial, badly organized searches. The scouring of 500 apartments was also delayed. No direct appeal was made to the kidnapper in the hours after the crime. It was left to Madeleine's distraught parents to publicly plea for help. There were no official posters of the missing child printed: locals and Mark Warner staff produced their own. The police even refused to distribute pictures of the missing child until 7th May. A complete list of guests at the resort was not compiled until two days after Madeleine went missing, meaning that many potential witnesses had already left. Police had not identified any suspects, despite having an e-fit of a man with long hair, which they refused to hand over to the media. The final blunder was that a detailed description of what the child was wearing was not issued. In fact, the Portuguese police maintained a wall of silence, claiming that privacy laws stopped them from revealing many details about their investigation. Detective Superintendent Alan Ladley, who had led the hunt for murdered 8-year-old Sarah Payne in 2000, said the blunders could be fatal. He added: "It's basic coppering... making sure your search doesn't miss vital clues that could crack the case, and checking on known and suspected sex offenders to see who's in the area." There were reports at this time that Madeleine could have been snatched by a British-led paedophile gang, one police source said: "The chance that Madeleine's kidnap was ordered by an international paedophile network of UK origin is one of the most consistent leads officers were investigating."

Meanwhile, Alan Ladley told Portuguese police: "The key is usually very nearby. Madeleine's disappearance seems to have been planned. This was not someone passing by and seizing an opportunity. This is someone who has been watching, even stalking, the family and knows all their movements."

On 11th May 2007, it was believed that Madeleine could have been snatched by two men and a woman in a British car, police believed. The three suspects were caught on CCTV at a petrol station near Praia da Luz, thus raising fears that she had been kidnapped by a gang who were "stealing to order". The lead came as Madeleine's parents released a new picture of their daughter in an Everton shirt. A police source said: "This CCTV footage from the garage was fed into the investigation after a worker expressed suspicions about the way the people were acting." Another witness was sure that one of the trio was the same man who had taken photos of his daughter on a nearby beach just three days earlier. Descriptions of the gang and the car's details were flashed to police around Europe by Interpol.

The investigation achingly stretched over the next few months. There were possible sightings, new leads and more witness statements than the police could handle. A woman had even spotted a man carrying a small child close to the McCann's apartment, but there was no news of what had happened to the now 4-year-old Madeleine McCann. Her birthday on 12th May came and went without her. It was marked with "prayer and contemplation". She had been missing for nine days at this point. Celebrity donations from the likes of J K Rowling, Sir Philip Green and Sir Richard Branson, Wayne Rooney and Simon Cowell had brought the reward money on offer for Madeleine's safe return to the region of £2.6 million. By 13th May 2007 there was an official news blackout, although it was confirmed that white vans were a new focus of attention at the resort after reports emerged of a man seen loitering in one outside the apartment where Madeleine disappeared. By 18th May, a website set up by the family had gained support from more than 25 million people worldwide. Meanwhile, Kate's bravery and dignity in the face of the most appalling loss touched the hearts of an entire nation, as she left a church service wearing a yellow ribbon in her hair in tribute to her daughter.

Witnesses continued to come forward, including a woman who said she had seen a blonde child matching Madeleine's description at a petrol station in Morocco two weeks after the child was kidnapped. The witness was unaware at the time that Madeleine had gone missing, but reported her sighting after she returned to the UK. Madeleine's family believed that she had been taken to North Africa. Meanwhile, two men, Robert Murat and Russian computer expert Sergey Malinka, became suspects in the case. Detectives were said to be concerned that although the two men claimed only to be business acquaintances, they had spoken to each other on the phone at 11.40pm on the night Madeleine went missing and had been caught on CCTV speaking animatedly in the days after the child vanished. Murat had also hired a car for the three days after the abduction; it was said that his own car had clutch problems. By 15th May, Murat was given *arguido* status (suspect) and the family's support website showed 58 million visitors. Murat had acted as an unofficial interpreter for the Portuguese police after Madeleine vanished. His ex-wife, Dawn, spoke out in his defence when he was held by police. She was utterly convinced that he was being made a scapegoat by police. She said: "I will always defend Robert because I know he would have nothing to do with something like this." But, Murat wasn't the only "suspect" to whom the Portuguese decided to give *arguido* status. In a shocking development, Kate and Gerry McCann were named as suspects by police and given the official status on 7th September 2007. By this time, there had been "no trace of evidence" linking Robert Murat to the kidnap of the little girl. The case against him had been on the "verge of collapse" as early as the end of May 2007. Between this time and the announcement of the McCanns' *arguido* status, the couple had been wracked with guilt over the disappearance of their daughter. It is one of the emotions that parents of abducted children are forced to confront.

As journalist Martin Fricker wrote, Kate and Gerry McCann "were cruelly forced to deny being involved in her kidnap". He continues: "In a shocking slur, German reporter Sabine Mueller asked 'How do you feel that more and more people seem to imply you might have something to do with it?'" The parents of Madeleine were appalled at the idea and a defiant Mueller said: "Either they're very good actors or they're telling the truth." It was one of a number of slurs that the McCanns were to face over the months since Madeleine's kidnap. The "outrageous question" asked by Mueller left the McCanns "visibly stunned", but despite their anger they kept their dignity. Mueller had asked the question of the McCanns and had deliberately mentioned the fact that people were saying their "cool and calm" behaviour was not the way people expected them to act – leading to rumours that the McCanns had been involved. Mueller was dubbed by British newspapers as "cruel". Then came the hoaxes – a man called from outside Europe saying he knew where Madeleine was being kept captive, while an anonymous letter claimed the little girl was buried nine miles from Praia da Luz. Next came accusations by the police that the McCanns had destroyed vital evidence by contaminating the crime scene as they frantically searched for their daughter just after she went missing. It was suggested by the British press that the Portuguese police were seen as trying to deflect attention away from their "bungling".

In June 2007, a string of tourists reported seeing Madeleine in Malta and a full-scale hunt was launched there after five separate sightings. Two of the tourists believed they had spoken to Madeleine on a bus in Malta. By this time there were 11 sightings. But, hopes in Malta faded after the police admitted that all investigations had drawn a blank. The McCanns stayed in Portugal – apart from visiting other European countries to publicize the search for their missing daughter.

Another suspect was former millionaire Danilo Chemello, who was held by police at the end of June 2007 for allegedly trying to extort £2.4 million from the fund set up to help find Madeleine and other children like her. Then came the startling news that the Portuguese police had decided that Madeleine could not have been kidnapped. They believed that the child had died in the family's holiday flat. A 50-page report was handed to prosecutors revealing "new and strong doubts" about the claims that Madeleine had been abducted. Meanwhile, Robert Murat left the police station after being quizzed again on 10th July 2007. He was still the only official suspect at this time. They still had no evidence to charge him.

At the end of July that same year, "Cracker-style" criminal profilers arrived in Portugal to aid the search. They were to take part in a detailed review of the then 89-day investigation. The hunt moved to Belgium in August when a man was wanted for questioning who had been seen with a woman and a girl resembling Madeleine. A drinking straw used by the little girl in a Belgian bar was then DNA tested. Although all the "sightings" of Madeleine renewed hope for her parents, the wait for confirmation, results and news was as agonizing as ever. In August 2007 blood specks found in the flat where Madeleine was snatched were hurriedly analysed to see if they were hers. The faint traces were discovered halfway up a wall, as highly trained British sniffer dogs examined the flat for the first time. Incredibly, the blood traces – that it appeared someone had tried to remove – lay undetected by Portuguese police for three months. The find came amid reports that the then sole suspect Robert Murat was about to be cleared.

Dozens of forensic samples that could have helped to find Madeleine were discovered by British police after being missed by Portuguese investigators. A senior source said: "It's staggering that three months into this investigation samples are still being recovered at the original crime scene." Meanwhile, the tests on the straw in Belgium proved inconclusive. By the middle of August, Kate and Gerry McCann were facing a smear campaign against them in Portugal. Kate said: "I'm not prepared to be bullied into doing something I don't want to. We will not be leaving. This speculation has been hurtful, intrusive and disrespectful. The last week has been particularly difficult, but we can cope with a lot and still have a lot of strength." In an astonishing attack, the lawyer for 33-year-old Brit, Robert Murat, claimed that locals wanted the "bloody McCanns" to leave the Portuguese resort. This was at the same time that cruel Portuguese reports continued to claim that the police were treating Kate and Gerry as suspects. The family were also asked to remove their two children, Sean and Amelie, from a local crèche because the constant press attention was affecting other families. Tearfully Kate said: "It's sticks and stones. But we'll never go through anything worse than being parted from Madeleine."

Meanwhile, Portuguese police came under further pressure for their "bungled" handling of the case, including the fact that they hadn't searched the garden of Robert Murat thoroughly enough. British officers had to carry out a second search. Police then further infuriated the McCanns by announcing – without their knowledge – that they thought Madeleine might be dead. It was particularly distressing for the missing child's family, who had been under immense pressure since the night she vanished. What with the rumours, speculation, knowledge that the police hadn't been working in the right way from the start, reported sightings, conjecture and having their other two children rejected due to the pressure it was putting on other families, the McCanns were being tested to the absolute limit. The wild claims that Madeleine had been killed and her body dumped in the sea added to her parents' enduring agony. They then demanded "showdown" talks with the Portuguese authorities. They were furious over the lack of information from the police. However, the entire case was put on hold while scientists in the UK tested the blood found at the flat. By this time, relations between the McCanns and the Portuguese police had completely broken down.

Police then announced on 21st August 2007 that more than one person was likely to have kidnapped Madeleine. They were hoping for a dramatic and imminent breakthrough in the case and, for the first time, Kate and Gerry were urged not to leave the country. There were reports that the police were going to arrest Dr Russell O'Brien, who was with the family on holiday when Madeleine went missing. Senior detectives told prosecutors that they believed Madeleine had been killed accidentally in the holiday flat – and they claimed to have evidence to support the theory. A source said: "All they would say is they have evidence her death was accidental. Nobody knows what the evidence is." The source added: "They don't think she was killed on purpose. At the moment they are leaning towards it being a tragic accident." There was then fury when TV reporter Sandra Felgueiras was alleged to have accused the McCanns of being involved in Madeleine's disappearance. She even suggested that Kate McCann could have murdered her own daughter. The McCanns were by this time convinced that Madeleine had been smuggled to Spain shortly after she was abducted. The couple were also attacked by Spanish interviewer, Jordi Gonzalez, who became more and more confrontational with Gerry on a TV broadcast, leading to Gerry furiously walking off the show. The Portuguese newspaper *Tal & Qual* was sued by the couple who launched a defamation case when the paper claimed that they had killed their daughter. A further blow came when the Portuguese police refused to tell them the results of the DNA testing on blood and other forensic evidence taken from the flat.

A *Mirror* article in September 2007 stated: "The stress of coping with the disappearance of a child would be hard enough for any parent – but Kate and Gerry McCann have also had to reckon with the slurs of Portugal's media." Local newspapers and TV stations had waged a relentless, hurtful and often bizarre smear campaign against them. Some of the accusations included that they were into wife swapping, that the couple had been bugged (by the police), that they had accidentally killed their child, that Gerry was not Madeleine's birth father, that the blood in the flat was Madeleine's, that the child had been sedated, that the McCanns had had a drunken party, that they had left the children while they went into Lagos one night – a 15-minute drive away – and that their friend, Dr O'Brien, had "mysteriously" disappeared for more than an hour on the night Madeleine went missing.

One of the ways in which Kate coped during this difficult time was to spend time "confiding her private hell" in a black ringbound diary. For the heartbroken mother, it was a small but vitally important way of helping her cope with the loss of her 4-year-old daughter. The diary was dragged into the police investigation in the hope that it would yield clues as to Kate's emotional state. Prosecutors applied to seize the diary as well as Gerry's laptop. They wanted to compare Kate's diary entries with her statements and her movements that had been given or were known to police. A week after being declared formal suspects by the police, the McCanns were back home in Rothley. Meanwhile, it was believed that Kate would be called by Portuguese prosecutors, accused of "accidental homicide". The family, however, believed they were being set up in order to cover up a bungled inquiry. Their Portuguese lawyer, Carlos Pinto de Abreu, blasted Portugal's judicial system saying: "Justice in Portugal is incapable of producing proof. It's more appropriate to break the reputation of an innocent man than to identify those responsible."

There were sensational claims in mid-September 2007 that Madeleine had died of a sleeping pill overdose. Body fluids found in the boot of a Renault Scenic rented by the McCanns allegedly proved that the child had been heavily sedated. The claim was made by French newspaper *Soir*, which said it had "hard evidence" to back this. Meanwhile, blood had been found by sniffer dogs in an apartment close to where Madeleine disappeared. Police believed that the little girl's body was hidden there. Sniffer dogs were known to have traced Madeleine from the family's flat to the apartment. Kate McCann had already been questioned for 11 hours before being named an *arguido*, but now it was believed that police would want to question her again. The friends on holiday with the family denied all rumours about Kate McCann as being a "hurtful" conspiracy. The wild theories continued – from the claim that Madeleine had been weighted with stones and dumped off a British-owned yacht, to Kate and Gerry having an accomplice who had disposed of the body for them. But the tide against Madeleine's parents was beginning to turn...

A judge in Portugal ruled that the McCanns did not need to return to the country, while Prime Minister Gordon Brown took a daily interest in their plight. On 18th September 2007 it was expected that a new spokesman for the couple, Clarence Mitchell, would declare them innocent. Meanwhile, a fourth Moroccan sighting of Madeleine came, after tourist Calra Torres was convinced she had seen the little girl in North Africa. However, the news that the little girl was not Madeleine came as a devastating blow to the McCanns. Clarence Mitchell told the press "enough is enough", after more slurs on the family came from the Portuguese press – including that Madeleine's body had been hidden in a fridge while the McCann's holiday friends were accused of a "pact of silence". Mitchell said: "It's just one ridiculous allegation after another, each is unsourced, unsubstantiated and unnamed..."

In October 2007, Robert Murat was once again questioned by police due to inconsistencies in his statements made in May that year. Meanwhile, another witness, Naoul Malhi, spotted a blonde girl with a bruised face being dragged along by a Moroccan woman. The child had a flecked iris, identical to Madeleine's. Naoul said: "It was Madeleine. There's no mistaking that mark." Before she could raise the alarm, however, the woman had bundled the child into a taxi and sped off.

In November, the evidence at that time was as follows: Jane Tanner provided the most crucial evidence when she saw a man carry a child from the McCanns' apartment at 9.15pm – 45 minutes before Kate raised the alarm. Dr Russell O'Brien was away from the group between 9.30pm and 10.15pm, tending his poorly daughter. He saw Robert Murat outside the McCann apartment that night, but Murat said he was at home with his mother. Dr Matthew Oldfield said he checked on the McCann children at 9.30pm but did not actually see Madeleine. He also saw Murat. Rachael Oldfield also saw Murat that night. Dr Fiona Payne also saw Murat. Having been the only one to possibly see Madeleine being abducted, Jane Tanner was filled with sorrow and "absolute horror" that perhaps she could have saved the little girl.

Portuguese police then announced in December 2007 that they had no proof that Madeleine was killed in the flat and had returned, once again, to the theory that she had been abducted. By the end of that month, a massive new poster campaign was launched in Morocco to help find the missing child. There had been numerous reports of Madeleine being sighted there. Private investigators were convinced she was abducted by a paedophile ring and smuggled by sea to North Africa. The family who had rented the holiday flat prior to the McCanns, and another British tourist, both said that they had seen a "creepy" stranger in the area who said he was collecting money for an orphanage. A witness Paul Gordon said he had spotted the man outside the patio doors where Madeleine disappeared (they were unlocked the night she went missing): the man was seen there just two weeks before the McCanns arrived, which raised suspicions as the doors were at the back of the building. Another witness, Gail Cooper, also saw the man – who gave the same excuse for his presence at her holiday villa. Meanwhile, private investigators claimed that Madeleine had been snatched by a Spanish paedophile ring and switched their probe to Valencia and Alicante. Jane Tanner and Gail Cooper both said that the man in the sketch of Madeleine's suspected kidnapper was the man they had seen. The sketch came in January 2008 and another witness, who claimed to have seen Madeleine in Morocco, said it was the same man she had seen with the child.

Kate and Gerry McCann were eventually cleared of any involvement and their *arguido* status was lifted on 21st July 2008. Robert Murat was also cleared at this time and his *arguido* status lifted. The disappearance of young Madeleine McCann remained in the media spotlight for the next five years and, in June 2012, Scotland Yard officers flew to Spain and Portugal as part of their investigations after Home Secretary Theresa May announced a review of the case by top British police. Detective Chief Inspector Andy Redwood, leading the UK hunt for the little girl, who would now be 9 years old, said: "We are here in terms of seeking to bring closure to the case. Closure means establishing what has happened to Madeleine." Portuguese police were also reviewing the clues.

Meanwhile, Madeleine's parents have suffered more than five years of heartache since she was kidnapped. A statement on their website on 24th April 2012 read: "Madeleine is still missing and someone needs to be looking for her. We love her dearly and miss her beyond words."

Shannon Matthews

(2008)

The bizarre case of what happened to Shannon Matthews meant that when investigating kidnaps and abductions of children in the future, the police would have to consider, sadly, whether the family of the victim was in any way involved in such a heinous crime. It is a sad reflection in the 21st century that this is exactly what happened to the 9-year-old from Dewsbury, West Yorkshire.

A desperate hunt for Shannon was launched in February 2008 when she vanished on her way home from school. As temperatures plummeted to minus 7°C the night she disappeared, police scored woodlands and broke the ice on a lake in the search for the timid girl who was afraid of the dark. It was revealed that Shannon had talked to friends about running away as her distraught mum, Karen, made a tearful appeal for her to return home. Chief Superintendent Barry South said: "Talks with Shannon's friends have revealed she had talked about running away. We are concerned about the cold weather and we're desperate to find her safe. Every hour counts at this stage." As darkness fell, the police search moved to flats near Shannon's home, where a cordon was put up and yellow cards marking evidence were scattered on the floor. Shannon disappeared after she was dropped off by coach at school following a trip to a swimming pool. The last confirmed sighting of her was at around 3.10pm as she left Westmoor Junior School. Her home was less than a mile away and classmate Chloe West, 8, said: "After we all got off the bus, Shannon went a different way to the rest of us and we don't know why. Someone said they thought they saw her crying earlier in the day." A fellow pupil claimed to have seen Shannon at around 7.30pm near the school's "top gates". More than 200 officers searched the estate and surrounding area where Shannon lived with her mum, Karen, 32, brothers Tony, 11, Cameron, 5, and sister Courtney, 18 months. A cousin of Karen's, Susan Howgate, described Shannon as: "a quiet girl, very shy", while her uncle, Neil Hyett, 36, said: "Shannon's a happy-go-lucky girl, not one for going about on the streets." Meanwhile, Shannon's father, Leon Rose, who was separated from Karen, said at his home in Huddersfield: "I'm just waiting on news and hoping she's OK."

On the third day that Shannon was missing, Detective Superintendent Andy Brennan said grimly: "I couldn't be more concerned for this young girl." There were fears that the 9-year-old had been abducted, or had run away and was simply too scared to come home again. But she had disappeared after telling friends that she had been wrongly accused of stealing from her mum's purse. It was also said that she was jealous of her older brother Tony and the attention he received, however, he himself had run away from home on numerous occasions. Instead of a "telling off", Tony was given a computer in the hope that he would "change his ways". Andy Brennan revealed that Shannon wasn't streetwise and was vulnerable. "Under normal circumstances we'd have expected to find her. That's why we're so concerned", he said. As

260 officers and more than 100 neighbours continued to hunt for Shannon, her distraught mother was comforted and supported by family liaison officers. Karen's partner, Craig Meehan, was not at home.

Just 20 minutes before she disappeared, pictures taken at the time showed a seemingly carefree Shannon chatting to a friend at the swimming baths after her lesson. The pictures were released by police as they admitted they "could not be more worried" for her safety. Officers showed the footage to Karen as they continued their house-to-house inquiries and said: "We're continuing the search process and are interviewing immediate family, friends and neighbours." Karen said that detectives had taken her live-in boyfriend Craig Meehan's mobile phone as a matter of routine. Meanwhile, Leon Rose said that Shannon had wanted to live with him. She had scrawled a message on her bedroom wall saying "I want to go and live with dad", just hours before vanishing. Tearful Karen said: "I noticed the writing after Shannon went missing. It was quite small and faint. I had no idea she felt like this, I didn't know anything was wrong." Karen added: "I've no idea why she would run away and I don't understand why she wanted to see Leon, because she thinks of Craig as a dad. She is much more of a daddy's girl than a mummy's girl and Craig and her spend lots of quality time together." Police searched the family home and spoke to her friends in the hope that it would solve the mystery. By 25th February, just seven days after Shannon disappeared, police had made painstaking searches of more than 200 homes, including a flat believed to have belonged to Karen's ex-boyfriend. All the properties within half a mile of the child's red-brick semi-detached home were searched. A spokeswoman from West Yorkshire police described the investigation as "extensive" and stressed that door-to-door inquiries were part of the wider hunt. She added: "This forms an important part of the investigation to build up a clearer picture of Shannon and her lifestyle." More than 300 calls had been made by members of the public, while worried neighbours and family members, some wearing T-shirts showing pictures of the schoolgirl, filled the residents' association hall near her home. Leaflets and posters appealing for information were distributed, and day and night searches by friends and relatives remained ongoing.

Shannon, described as 4ft 1in, slim with shoulder-length medium-brown hair and blue eyes and freckles, was dressed in a black jumper with a school logo on it, a white cotton T-shirt, black trousers and a waist-length black coat with fur around the hood. She was also wearing distinctive pink and grey Bratz furry boots. On 26th February, Karen and her boyfriend Craig Meehan were allowed to return to their home after police finished searching it, but the anguished mother couldn't bear to go back. A friend, Peter Brown, said: "Both Craig and Karen are beside themselves and still can't bear to go back home." He continued: "They're still hoping and praying she is found safe and well." Police meanwhile continued their search, but found no links to the case. Chief Superintendent Barry South said: "We are looking round the area that Shannon frequented. I believe somebody out there has a vital piece of information." By 27th February the police felt that Shannon "may have fallen into the wrong hands". Detective Superintendent Andy Brennan spoke of his "grave concerns" as he confirmed that his team was using sniffer dogs trained to seek out human remains. After officers completed a search of a house belonging to the 9-year-old's uncle, DS Brennan said:

"I'm convinced that if Shannon had run away of her own volition we would have found her by now – over a week on from when the investigation opened. In searches of this kind, it is very rare that a girl of Shannon's age should be missing for this long without any clues pointing to her whereabouts. It is extremely concerning. We are now looking at this on a scale as serious as a murder investigation. It can be said the tone of our inquiry has changed to a bleaker outlook. No arrests have been made at this point, and I must stress that we are not ruling out any possibilities as to what might have happened to her."

A dozen officers wearing white masks searched the property next door to Shannon's family home – of her uncle, Neil Hyett, and his wife Amanda. They rummaged through rubbish in the garden and all the dustbins in the street. Later in the afternoon, eight police officers searched and photographed the home of friend and neighbour Peter Brown, and continued their search of more than 2,000 homes, looking at "key individuals" and following a number of leads. Meanwhile, police confirmed the attempted abduction of a 12-year-old girl in nearby Wakefield, also called Shannon. A man tried to get the girl into his car and then chased her on foot, allegedly on the same day that her namesake disappeared 10 miles away in Dewsbury. Police were not necessarily linking the two cases, although due to the proximity of the two incidents, they were not ruling out a connection.

Karen, meanwhile, said she would never stop searching for her daughter. Fighting back tears, she said: "We will never give up on her. It is more than a week and we are desperate to have Shannon back. Our message to people is never give up because we won't." Peter Brown's home, where Karen and Craig had been staying, was searched for a second day while sniffer dogs searched wasteland, gardens and homes in Dewsbury.

Hundreds of well-wishers marched through Dewsbury behind a "Help Find Shannon" picture banner. Accompanied by Karen and Craig, the crowd then released balloons and laid flowers at the couple's home. Karen said: "We've shed a lot of tears. It was really emotional seeing people walking through the streets with us to support our family. I was overwhelmed by the turnout. Now we just want Shannon found. We just pray she will be found safe." Craig said: "People have been fantastic. We want to thank everyone."

Meanwhile, at the beginning of March, as Shannon's family prepared to face Mothering Sunday without her, her friend Megan revealed how she had told police that Shannon was angry with the bullies at school who kicked her. She made an emotional appeal to her friend saying: "Please come home Shannon, we all miss you. If anyone knows where Shannon is they should tell."

Karen, clutching a posy of flowers from her other children, spent Mothering Sunday on 2nd March 2008 being comforted by friends and family. In a statement, she said:

"Mother's Day is a day when every mum wants her children around them. Today I don't want cards or presents, I just want my darling daughter home safely. I know Shannon would normally have made me a Mother's Day card at school and we would have spent the day together. I feel sure that she is alive and will come home to her mum. If anyone knows where Shannon is, please think about my family this Mother's Day and bring my beautiful princess home where she belongs with her mum, dad, brothers and little sister."

As Craig vowed never to give up the hunt for Shannon, specially trained body-finding dogs were brought in to search fields behind her home. But they found nothing. One police officer said: "She has vanished into thin air." In early March, Karen told how she feared that her daughter had been snatched by someone close to the family. Asked who she thought might be responsible, Karen Matthews wept: "I think somebody out there knows Shannon and who probably knows me as well. It makes me think I can't trust people who are really close to me any more." She also gave police her blessing to carry out criminal checks on family and friends. She spoke of how the youngster's disappearance on 19th February had "wreaked a devastating emotional toll on the family". The tormented mum – clutching her daughter's favourite teddy and wearing a T-shirt with the slogan "Help Find Shannon" said: "Somebody out there who has got Shannon has broken the family we had apart. The family don't feel safe any more." "However", wrote *Mirror* reporter Lucy Thornton, "Karen clings to the belief that her daughter, although in the clutches of an abductor, is still alive. And in a heartrending plea direct to the possible kidnapper, she begged: 'I feel someone has got Shannon. If you have Shannon please let her go.'"

The news – or rather non-news – about Shannon continued throughout the first week of March. Even the boyband Westlife, the child's favourite group, made an emotional plea to help find her. Her best friend, Megan, was lonely and upset with no one to play with at school and was also fearful that the little girl she'd been "bestest friends" with for two years was never coming home. A psychic claimed that Shannon had been taken by a man who knew both Karen and her daughter "vaguely" when he told the anguished mother that he believed the child was still alive and being held by the man. By this point, more than 300 detectives and police – 10 per cent of the West Yorkshire force – were involved in the investigation. Meanwhile, Leon Rose looked everywhere he could think of for his daughter. He put up posters, pleaded with anyone who could help to do so and even leapt to the defence of Shannon's beleaguered "stepdad" Craig Meehan. As Meehan fiercely rejected claims that he hit 9-year-old Shannon, her birth father said: "I've always thought he was a decent guy." Leon was speaking amid allegations that Meehan was a cruel dad, after Shannon's grandmother, June Matthews, claimed that "he was a sinister presence in the family home". June told journalists: "Karen was a great mum before she took Craig in. Those kids were loved and cared for. Since he arrived, they've had a terrible time." By this time, more than half the country's sniffer dogs were involved in the hunt for the missing child, while on 12th March 2008, Karen claimed that someone may have abducted Shannon "just to hurt me". The mother of seven – of whom three of her children live with their fathers – said that officers leading the hunt said she would have to prove that as a theory. She also again denied allegations that Craig Meehan had hit her daughter.

Mick Donovan, 39, became a suspect in the kidnap case when it was revealed that he had sexually abused two boys. He was said to have made the brothers, aged 6 and 12, fondle each other. He abused the two boys and preyed on them while living with their unsuspecting family. At the time, Donovan was known by his real name – Paul Drake. Both brothers stated how dangerous Donovan was and the police quizzed the "oddball" about Shannon's kidnap. The abuse of the two brothers, which had happened 13 years earlier, had brought back terrible memories for them. Donovan's two daughters, aged 10 and 12 at the time he was brought in for questioning, were said to be in and out of care after he split from their mother. Donovan – aka Paul Drake – was Craig Meehan's uncle.

When police eventually found Shannon Matthews in Donovan's house, 24 days after she went missing, it was claimed that the child did not know she had been kidnapped. The disclosure came as it emerged that the 9-year-old was asked if she wanted to return home, or not. Social workers and police were gently quizzing her about every aspect of her life. It was believed that so far no evidence of sexual abuse had been discovered after she was plucked from the suspect's flat. Jubilant Karen Matthews waited for a reunion with her daughter, while police said: "It's unlikely that Shannon will be coming home today. That decision will be made by people working closely with her. We're pretty certain Shannon will have some say in that." Shannon was found in Donovan's flat, just one mile from her home. Donovan's family went into hiding, ashamed that one of their relatives – despite the fact they'd had very little to do with him – was involved in Shannon's abduction.

On 18th March 2008 it was revealed that Shannon would not be returning to her mum and Craig, but would be looked after by specialist carers. She would not be going home just yet. Karen said: "I find it very hard because I can't hold her or cuddle her."

Detectives Paul Kettlewell and Nick Townsend had refused to leave when they got no answer at Donovan's flat, where neighbours said they could hear a child's footsteps. They watched the front and back entrances and called for a battering ram. They broke down the door and discovered Shannon. She was found hidden in a divan bed. For the detectives, it was the 700th action they had taken since the start of the investigation and had made inquiries of the neighbours. Both were highly praised by Chief Constable Sir Norman Bettison for their dedication in finding Shannon. Bettison said: "She's in the hands of people who can be trusted to do everything that is possibly needed for her welfare and care." Meanwhile, back home in Dewsbury, Karen and Craig were trying to cope without her.

Six weeks after she vanished, Shannon Matthews was reunited with her mum, Karen, on 2nd April 2008. The emotional meeting took place at a secret address after Craig Meehan was arrested for allegedly having child pornography on a computer. For four weeks, Shannon had been living with foster carers. Speaking about Craig, Karen said: "I'm in shock. I just can't say anything." Shortly after his arrest, Karen went with friends and their children to an Easter egg hunt in a local park. From there she was collected by police for the secret meeting with her daughter. There were still some unanswered decisions to be made about the girl's future.

Craig Meehan's mother and sister were charged with child pornography offences and were arrested on 4th April 2008. Craig's sister, Amanda Hyett (who was married to Karen's brother) was arrested on suspicion of assisting an offender, while their mother, Alice, was arrested on suspicion of attempting to pervert the course of justice. The dramatic developments came after Karen Matthews was forced to flee her home following death threats. She had dumped Craig Meehan and was in hiding at a secret address.

The next dramatic twist came when kidnap suspect Donovan slit his wrists in a suicide attempt while in prison. Wardens raised the alarm after finding the former computer programmer. It was not known at this stage what weapon he used. Donovan was taken to hospital for emergency treatment but was returned to prison in Leeds, where he was on remand. He had been charged with kidnap and false imprisonment of the 9-year-old. But, the drama continued when Karen Matthews was arrested after allegedly telling friends: "I knew where she was." She was thought to have said she was about to leave partner Craig Meehan after being offered a place to stay by the man accused of the 9-year-old's kidnap. On 7th April 2008 she was quizzed on suspicion of perverting the course of justice. It was then revealed that it was believed that Shannon's disappearance was linked to a cash scam. The theory emerged as police asked for a copy of an episode from the TV show *Shameless* in which a fake kidnap was staged and a £50,000 ransom paid. The TV "victim" was hidden a few doors down the same street in which he lived, staying with a friend of his sister. The episode was screened just one month before Shannon went missing.

Karen allegedly announced that she had known where Shannon was being held while waiting at traffic lights in an unmarked police car with a family liaison officer, Detective Constable Christine Freeman and two neighbours. The 32-year-old was thought to have told how she was planning to leave Meehan – even packing a plastic bag of clothes – and had been offered a place to stay by Donovan.

Shannon had been found in the flat in Batley Carr, West Yorkshire, on 14th March. Three days later, Donovan was charged with kidnap and false imprisonment of the child. On 2nd April Meehan was arrested, while his mother and sister were arrested two days later. Just two days after that, on 6th April, Karen Matthews was arrested.

The police even investigated whether Shannon's family had tried to con cash out of Kate and Gerry McCann. People claiming to be related to Shannon rang or wrote several times asking for money from the Find Madeleine fund. Kate and Gerry wanted to help, but others became suspicious and refused. A spokesperson for the Find Madeleine fund confirmed: "No money exchanged hands. The idea was discussed by the fund's directors. However, others were concerned about the haphazard method of approach and suggested we did not get involved."

By 14th April, as Karen remained in jail on remand, it was revealed that vengeful inmates had offered a packet of cigarettes to the first to beat her up. A source said: "I've friends inside and they reckon she's in for a right beating." Karen was said to be in constant tears at New Hall women's jail near Wakefield. Karen was charged with perverting the course of justice and child neglect. She was put in a single cell where she spent up to 20 hours a day on her own, worrying about the beating she was threatened with.

For 24 days, a dingy bedroom with threadbare carpets and dirty walls was the most hunted hideaway in Britain. Day in and day out, increasingly worried police drew a blank as they looked for the 9-year-old in the biggest search since the Yorkshire Ripper. The youngster was being held against her will in a two-bedroom top-floor flat rented by Mick Donovan. The scruffy bedroom containing cheap wooden furniture was the former room of Donovan's two daughters who had gone into care. Shannon, two months after her ordeal ended, was still suffering nightmare hallucinations. Meanwhile, her mother was due to go on trial alongside the alleged kidnapper of her daughter. Karen Matthews appeared in court accused of perverting the course of justice and repeatedly concealing information as the police tried to trace the child. Also facing a charge of willful child neglect, Matthews appeared in Leeds crown court via video link from New Hall Prison. Sitting on a chair and wearing a sky-blue T-shirt under a grey zipped top, she spoke only to confirm her name and that she could hear the proceedings. Judge Peter Collier told her that she would stand trial on 11th November 2008 alongside Donovan, charged with kidnap and false imprisonment. On 18th April, Matthews was said to be in fear of her life as fellow prisoners warned: "We're going to get you! It's only a matter of time."

Police then confirmed – on 18th April 2008 – that Matthews had been charged for a second time in connection with her daughter's disappearance, alongside Meehan and Donovan who were both charged with perverting the course of justice. The fund containing thousands of pounds donated by well-wishers during the hunt for Shannon was to go to two children's charities. Meehan was convicted of child pornography and went into hiding in September 2008 after residents in Dewsbury told him to stay away for good. He was found guilty of having 49 pictures of abuse on his computer, ranging from Level 1 to Level 4 (Level 5 is the worst). Some of the images were described by the judge as "stomach churning". Meehan was ordered to sign the sex offenders' register. Returning to the kidnap case, the court heard on 12th November 2008 how Shannon Matthews had been snatched and tied up with a noose in a "wicked" plot created by her own mother in order to make cash. Karen Matthews had arranged for Michael Donovan to entice the 9-year-old to visit a fair. But instead, she was drugged with sleeping pills and held for 24 days in his scruffy flat in Batley Carr. Jurors were told how Matthews had played the distraught mum as the reward money for her daughter's return rose to her £50,000 target. Prosecutor Julian Goose said: "This plan was... wicked." Shannon was tethered with a noose in the dingy flat, rather than going on the trip to the fair she had been enticed with. The court also heard how Karen Matthews hatched the plot with Donovan to kidnap the child and that they would only release her once a reward offered by a newspaper reached £50,000. Over the three weeks of her captivity, Shannon was kept prisoner and given a list of rules that were perched on top of the TV, which included staying away from the windows and keeping noise down. While she was shut away, Donovan went about his usual business. When the police raided Donovan's flat they discovered the noose and the list of rules, sedatives and a copy of a downmarket newspaper offering the reward. Julian Goose, QC, told the jury: "Police discovered a long strap, knotted on to the roof beam. It had a large loop at the end which, at full stretch, would reach around the flat but not permit anyone, restrained by it, from leaving through the front door." He told the court that Matthews and Donovan had come up with the plan over a drink in a cafe. Their plan was to imprison Shannon then release her in Dewsbury market. Donovan would then say he found her wandering around, take her to a police station and claim the reward.

The massive hunt for Shannon was one of Britain's biggest and left the police with a £3.2 million bill. After officers rammed the front door of Donovan's flat to gain entry, Shannon was found hidden in the base of a divan bed. She said "You're frightening me", when the police entered the flat and tipped up the bed in the search. Donovan was found hiding in the other half of the bed base. Donovan struggled with the police and was restrained. In the police van after his arrest he apparently said: "Get Karen down here, we'd got a plan." The tears of Karen Matthews as she pleaded for the return of her kidnapped child were part of a cruel charade, the jury heard. It was nothing but an act for the cameras, they were told. On 12th November, the jury were shown TV appeals made by the accused, day after day, begging for the return of her daughter. They were even shown footage of her direct pleas to her daughter's "abductor". But the jury were told she was "acting" all along as part of a plan to get £50,000 reward money. Julian Goose stated: "She conjured up tears in an effort to convince her audience that she was telling the truth, when it was a barefaced lie. She maintained the lie in the face of the substantial police work employed to try to find Shannon. The prosecution say that Karen Matthews is a consummate and convincing liar."

The jury also heard how Donovan, after his contact rights to his own daughter were stopped, had been charged with abducting the 11-year-old from outside her school while she was in foster care, and taking her to Blackpool where he had booked a B&B under false names.

In court on 4th December 2008, Karen Matthews was branded "pure evil" as it was revealed that the plot to kidnap her daughter

Shannon was inspired by the hunt for Madeleine McCann. Matthews and Donovan were facing substantial jail terms for keeping Shannon drugged and tethered in Donovan's flat, yet even before the kidnap, the schoolgirl had endured a life of torment and beatings at the hands of her mother. Shannon was often banished to her room with a packet of crisps for tea. She daren't complain, as she revealed in a poignant note to her brother, "'cos we'll be beaten". Police chief Andy Brennan also revealed how the drugs that Shannon was given by her captors to keep her quiet could have killed her. She was plied with five different drugs – including powerful antidepressants – for at least 20 days. DS Andy Brennan said: "It beggars belief that a mother would put her own child in this position. Shannon's lucky to be alive." He also said that the Madeleine McCann case was still fresh in everybody's minds and this is what gave Matthews and Donovan the idea. Matthews showed no emotion as she was found guilty at Leeds Crown Court of kidnap, false imprisonment and perverting the course of justice. Donovan sat slumped forward, staring at the floor as the jury gave their verdict after just six hours. DS Brennan said: "Karen Matthews is pure evil. It's difficult to understand what type of mother would subject her daughter to such a wicked crime. Shannon has been totally betrayed by her own mother." Even Matthews' sister Julie Poskitt agreed: "She's a bad mother. She'd think nothing of belting her kids or having a go. She's a disgrace."

One of the poignant notes written between Shannon and one of her brothers reads: "Do you think we'll get any tea tonight? *We may get a packet of crisps if we keep quiet.* Don't say anything 'cos we'll be beaten." The note was written by the two youngsters as they huddled together banished in the dark. After her rescue, Shannon was asked by child psychologists whether she wanted to go home. The reply came immediately – NO. It was then revealed that during her early years, Shannon had been placed on the "at risk" register by social services after her nursery headteacher warned care professionals on six occasions that Shannon was "dirty and neglected". A neighbour had alerted officials about the family on three occasions, but social services nevertheless eventually took Shannon off the "at risk" list. Karen Matthews had given cause for concern to outsiders because her children suffered violence, poor conditions, lack of control and poor school attendance. A psychologist's report, commissioned by social services on Matthews' parenting style in December 2003, concluded that she had an inability to put her children's needs above her own.

During the entire time that Shannon was missing, journalist Lucy Thornton had dedicated her time to covering the story and was with Karen Matthews an hour before the police found her daughter. She writes:

"During Shannon's 24-day kidnap I had spoken to Karen – always through a fog of cigarette smoke – several times. She used to mumble one-word answers to my questions as she sat in her dirty lounge packed with supportive neighbours. Despite the madness around her, she calmly watched the television – *Dora the Explorer* was her favourite show. Craig, meanwhile, sat sulking at the computer ignoring everybody. But my final chat with Karen took place in the Dewsbury Moor community house on 14th March. She was alone and finally revealed to me the real Karen, the vulgar, selfish and uncaring Karen. She boasted of getting drunk the night before, howled at dirty jokes and flirted with neighbours as she basked in her celebrity attention. But this stopped suddenly when Craig appeared and she returned to the guise of mourning mum. The pair were barely talking after a ferocious drunken row the night before but started holding hands when the *Mirror* photographer arrived. Karen then launched into a bizarre attack on her own mum June, blaming her for Shannon's disappearance…"

Meanwhile, a probe into the role of social services in the case of Shannon Matthews was welcomed. The serious case review would look at all the dealings social workers had with the family before Shannon was kidnapped. The probe came after a request by government minister Shahid Malik, the then MP for Dewsbury.

Receiving benefits of up to £240 per week, due to her wicked kidnap plot Karen Matthews became, at the end of 2008, the most reviled and scorned woman in Britain. But, to Meehan, jailed for downloading child pornography images, she was "the perfect woman and his dream lover", wrote journalist Lucy Thornton. For Matthews, however, it was known that Meehan was just another man in a long line of relationships undertaken by Shannon's mother as a way of having babies and taking money from the state in benefits. Even Matthews' sister said that Karen used the money given to her to buy nappies to instead fund her cigarettes and cider. However, social services were cleared on any wrongdoing – because the Serious Case Review said they could not have known or anticipated the kidnapping of Shannon. Lucy Thornton wrote:

"But I am not the only one to have been appalled by Karen's home life. Over the years teachers, police and neighbours had all alerted social services to the plight of her kids. People talked of carrier bags and tea towels used as nappies, her passion for teenage boys, letting paedophiles stay in her home and propping up her baby's milk bottle with cushions so the tots could feed themselves while she watched TV. Sex was a constant topic of conversation in front of anyone – including her own children."

The piece concludes: "but when Britain's worst mum was informed that she might lose her kids, she told a pal: 'Who cares? I'll just have another baby.'" Both Matthews and Donovan were sentenced to eight years for the ordeal they put Shannon through.

In 2012, Karen Matthews was released from prison after having served half her original sentence. In October 2012, Shannon's father, Leon Rose, battled for a report into Shannon's abduction to be blocked, over fears that it would upset his then teenage daughter. Leon Rose's lawyer claimed it would cause too much pain for her. The Kirklees Safeguarding Children Board report would re-examine Shannon's 24-day captivity, but Mr Rose wanted its publication halted so that his daughter could grow up as a normal teenager. Anthony Hayden, QC, told the High Court: "Nothing can prevent the upheaval that will be caused by it.". For Shannon, the child who went through such a terrible betrayal and ordeal, it can only be hoped that she can move forward with a life free from fear and abuse, and a life surrounded by those who truly love, support and care for her.

April Jones

(2012)

Five-year-old April Jones became the centre of a police search on 1st October 2012 when it was feared that she'd been snatched off the street. Officers swamped the area near her home after reports that the youngster was seen getting into a light-coloured van. April had been last seen on her bike by playmates at around 7.30pm close to her home on the Bryn-Y-Gog estate in Machynlleth, Wales. A spokesperson for Dyfed Powys police said: "We are increasingly concerned for missing five-year-old April, who was last seen playing on her bike. April was seen getting into a light-coloured van that drove off." Locals were also involved in the hunt and one said: "Pretty much the whole town is out looking. Other local towns are joining in as well." It was also reported that vehicles leaving the town were being stopped by police.

Detectives leading the search for April knew that the decisions they made could mean the difference between life and death. The investigation had had the best possible start, in that the fact that April was missing was immediately reported to the police, who straightaway launched a major criminal investigation. Officers were then faced with carrying out three simultaneous inquiries based on the three most obvious hypotheses. The first and most likely was that April had been kidnapped. By 2nd October 2012 a 46-year-old man was being quizzed and a vehicle was being examined by police. He could have been linked to the vehicle, or he could have been known to police and under surveillance. What the police really needed at that stage was the registration of the van described by April's young playmate. They began making inquiries and checking CCTV footage across the region. They were also checking all known child sex offenders in the area. The second theory was that April was lost and vulnerable. This could have overlapped with the first theory, in that the kidnapper for some reason had abandoned her. The final hypothesis was that she had been harmed by an individual known to her. There had been several cases where fears of abduction were wrong – ranging from the bizarre case of Shannon Matthews to the tragic murder of Tia Sharp in New Addington, south London. As a result, a senior officer had to arrange to search the houses of family and friends while sensitively interviewing relatives to eliminate the possibility of any family involvement. What detectives were really hoping for – besides finding the small child alive and well – was the chance that information would come to light to confirm which hypothesis they were actually dealing with.

It was also revealed around this time that April's best friend had begged her not to get into the van in which she was driven off by a kidnapper. As police and neighbours continued the hunt for the missing 5-year-old, an RAF search-and-rescue helicopter was scrambled to a "very specific location" at short notice with police on board. Meanwhile, 25-year-old mother of two, Vicky Fenner, told how the two close friends had been playing together when the kidnapper struck. She added: "The two girls went out together and we've been told by the 7-year-old that April got into a vehicle parked behind the garages. It was wet and cold and the other girl told April not to get into it. But April said: 'It's all right, I know them.' I think the girl was the only person who was with April. She is the last person to see her." Vicky Fenner also said that she had been told that April had been in the same vehicle two or three days before the kidnapping and that three children got into the vehicle, although one girl denied this. April's friend had said that she had willingly climbed into the left-hand drive van. The arrested man was named locally as Mark Bridger, a swimming pool attendant, who was reported to have a daughter around April's age (he is actually a father of six children). He was picked up while walking on a road near the town and police later found his vehicle nearby and took it for examination.

April's devastated parents, 40-year-old Coral and 43-year-old Paul, said in a statement directed at whoever had taken their daughter: "Please, if you have our little girl, let her come home to us." Shocked residents on the Mid Wales estate where April was snatched told how their quiet community had been shattered by the abduction. They also said that there had previously been no fears about letting children play outside, because the area was considered very safe. Vicky added: "I've grown up on this estate and we all thought this was the safest place in the world for kids to play. April goes past my house 20 times a day with her friend. This is such a shock because everybody looks out for everyone else's children and we all know what is going on." Another mother said: "We always thought this was the best place in the world to bring up kids. This is like taking the innocence away from our town. April is tiny and so sweet. It's shocking isn't it? They are a nice, normal family." While residents close to April's home were being interviewed by journalists and helping in the investigation and search, the police, coastguard, mountain rescuers and the RAF were concentrating their search for the little girl along the banks of a river. Powys Chief Superintendent Reg Bevan, leading the hunt for the child, who was wearing her favourite purple knee-length coat when she disappeared, said: "April is still missing and all lines of inquiry are continuing with the view she is alive." Officers had carefully quizzed April's friends to piece together the moments before she was snatched and to get a description of the kidnapper. Superintendent Ian John confirmed that the main witness was a 7-year-old. He added: "She saw her walking willingly into the van on the driver's side. We are treating the witness with a great deal of sensitivity and specialist officers trained to deal with children are slowly and precisely interviewing her." CS Bevan added: "The indications are that April got into the vehicle willingly. There's nothing to suggest at this stage there was a struggle." A report in the *Mirror* read: "April lives with her parents, sister Jasmine, 16, and brother Harley, aged nine." A neighbour of the family told how 45 minutes after April vanished, Coral turned up at his house in tears asking: "Have you seen my daughter?" He added: "Coral was totally distraught. She was in pieces. This is totally shocking. We come from a quiet Mid Wales town. We wanted to do anything to help. The way everyone has stepped up is amazing." Another mum who joined the hunt for the missing child said: "It is very scary and I can't even imagine what Coral and Paul are going through. It's heart-wrenching and horrible."

More than 500 people joined the police to help in the search in early October. They spent the night scouring every road within a 25-mile radius of the town. Helen Roberts described how 9-year-old Harley had banged on her door pleading for help after his sister went missing. She said he was in tears and he was frantic. Helen, a school dinner supervisor, described April as "a lovely, pretty little girl". She said: "I held her hand in the playground on Monday [the day April disappeared]. She said, 'What time's dinner, Auntie Helen?'" The 43-year-old also said that everybody was confused about where April could have been taken and by whom. Meanwhile, April's godmother, Mair Raftree, joined the hunt for the small child and said: "She is such an intelligent child there is no way she would get into a car with a stranger. She had to have known him. I cannot believe what is happening, no one can, we're in a state of shock and we are all praying for a miracle." Neighbours also confirmed that Bridger was well known in the small town. The *Mirror* joined one of the first of 20 search teams in the town's leisure centre at first light, stuffing pictures of April into their waterproof jackets before braving the wind and the rain.

The small, but willing army of volunteers set out in driving rain to scour Machynlleth and its surrounding countryside for the little girl who had simply vanished. Within a few minutes the 12-strong party, including journalist Luke Traynor, stopped as a pile of clothes was spotted lying in undergrowth close to a sports field. But the red jumper and blue trousers didn't appear to fit the description of "white primary school T-shirt, a purple padded coat with fur collar and black trousers" circulated by police. Even so, the find was documented and details passed back to a central chain of command back at the leisure centre. Geraint Evans, 37, was one of the lead organizers of the rescue effort after gathering a group of friends from Dovey Valley Motor Club. He said: "We know the local area well because we set up car rallies. We co-ordinated 250 people in the first search until 2am. When dawn broke it was the same again. The people have been so willing to help any way they can." Guy Haley, 29, was working on a road-widening project near the town. He described how as soon as April went missing his boss said they could stop work and help if they wanted. He said: "I've not stopped searching since." Any object or item spotted lying in the undergrowth was greeted with hope. But after two hours with no luck all the teams trudged back to the centre of Machynlleth, sodden, downhearted and with fears even blacker than when they had left.

On 3rd October, police were studying the picture of a man by a river near where kidnap suspect Mark Bridger was arrested. The shot was taken by a TV crew shortly before officers held the 46-year-old. Volunteers looking for April claimed that they saw Bridger walking on the bank minutes before the footage of the man fitting his description was taken at 1.45pm on Tuesday 2nd October by a Channel 4 news team. It is believed that the man asked one of the searchers if they had heard any news about the hunt for April. Bridger was held as he walked along a roadside near the Dyfi Bridge in Machynlleth and detectives were studying the image in the search for further clues about the youngster's abduction. The dramatic development came as detectives refused to rule out the possibility that the kidnapper was not working alone. Officers were probing the possibility that the abductor may have confided in a conspirator or another individual who might have known where the child was hidden. Superintendent Ian John said: "We are keeping an open mind." The police had taken the unusual step of naming Bridger as the man they arrested over April's disappearance at 3.30pm on Tuesday 2nd October. On 3rd October, they were given an extra 12 hours to question him. They said he was "wearing a camouflage jacket, black over trousers and camouflage trousers" when held. He had been interviewed twice by detectives but had not at this stage been charged with any offence.

As the hunt for April continued, 250 specialist officers were scouring more than 20 sites. Leading search experts were called in to help in terms of search management. Three experts from the Police National Search Centre and the Crime Operational Support Unit were asked to join the teams in Machynlleth. Police confirmed:

"There are a large number of sites. They are very varied and require a considerable amount of planning to ensure we achieve the most effective outcome. The geography is very challenging and everyone is working in a hostile environment, by that I mean, the terrain is difficult, waterlogged, working near to flooded rivers with the potential for mine shafts and unstable ground."

Police also said that there were a variety of buildings and open area searches which required flexibility and systematic methods to the operation. Superintendent Ian John said that the scale of the investigation was "unprecedented". He continued: "We've got over 100 mountain rescue experts, 100 police-trained search officers, 20 dog handlers, two vessels to search the river, a team of kayakers, as well as a marine unit." One of the volunteers who helped in the initial search was Bridger's son, Scott Williams, 19, who revealed that he had been estranged from his father for most of his life and had only met him a couple of months before April's disappearance. He said: "He has never been in my life. I only met him a couple of times down the local pub. It was a shock when we heard he'd been arrested." Meanwhile, Mair Raftree confirmed that April had had a medical condition since she was a baby and that the child needed daily medication and regular hospital checks. For April's parents, Coral and Paul, the continuing hunt and the absence of their daughter meant pure agony.

Family members were getting desperate and frustrated that such a massive search operation had found nothing. They were also baffled that Bridger was in custody, yet the police seemed no closer to finding April.

Coral Jones broke down in tears as she pleaded for help to find her daughter. Trembling with emotion and barely able to speak, April's mother told a press conference: "It is 36 hours since April was taken from us. There must be someone out there who knows where she is and can help the police find her. We are desperate for any news. April is only 5 years old – please, please help us find her." Coral's heart-rending appeal came as it was revealed that her daughter has a mild form of cerebral palsy for which she needed daily medication. A police spokesperson said: "This is a sensitive family issue but it is something we are aware of." Coral was led away sobbing after her first public appearance since April was snatched. Meanwhile, police issued a picture of ex-soldier Bridger, following his arrest on 2nd October. Detective Superintendent Reg Bevan appealed for information from anyone who had seen Bridger or the vehicle between Monday 1st October in the evening and Tuesday afternoon, and forensic officers searched a farmhouse where the suspect had been living since September 2012. It was thought that he had moved to the hamlet of Ceinws, five miles north of Machynlleth, after splitting with his girlfriend, Vicky Fenner (interviewed by newspapers shortly after April went missing). They also searched nearby factory units, farm buildings and forest shacks. It then transpired that two women claimed they had seen a man carrying a black bin-bag towards the River Dyfi the day after April Jones was snatched.

They told police that the man had scrambled down a bank not far from where the 5-year-old was snatched, leading officers to trawl the river. One of the women had been standing by a road chatting with a friend on Tuesday 2nd October when the man appeared with the black bag. He was described as acting suspiciously. All April's parents could do was wait.

On 5th October 2012, reports that a witness had seen a car speeding away from where April vanished were published in the newspapers. The distraught neighbour, 70, said that moments earlier he had noticed the 5-year-old playing near her home as a driver cruised around the area. Then April suddenly disappeared. He was the last person, apart from April's 7-year-old friend, to see her alive – as the hunt for the young girl was announced as a murder inquiry. The pensioner told how he was filled with anguish at what he had seen and the fact that he did not raise the alarm earlier. Police now feared that it was unlikely April Jones would be found alive. The neighbour, who wished to remain anonymous, said:

"I was home on Monday night as usual and saw little April playing outside with her friends. They were riding their bikes up and down the street like they have been all summer. A driver kept cruising up and down the road where the kids were playing. I thought it was a little odd but nothing more and then I noticed it parked up next to garages, which was strange because no one would park there usually. The kids were still playing at that point. But suddenly they weren't there and I noticed the car drive briskly down the road towards the town centre. To be honest I thought nothing of it until people started banging on my door about half an hour later asking if I'd seen April. Then I realized the significance of what I'd seen."

The witness spoke as detectives continued to quiz Bridger over the kidnapping. By now he was also suspected by police of the little girl's murder. It was the moment everyone had been dreading – that the hunt for April Jones would turn into a murder inquiry. As the news filtered through, those searching the area stood around in stunned disbelief. Some sobbed openly while others tearfully hugged friends and loved ones, seeking a shred of comfort in a very dark and desperate hour. Shortly before 10am on 5th October everything changed when the police revealed that ex-soldier Mark Bridger, 46, held for three days over her disappearance, had been arrested on suspicion of the 5-year-old's murder. He remained in custody after appearing in court where police sought a warrant to detain him for longer. By the time the news that Bridger was arrested on suspicion of murder was made public, April's parents had already been informed that her disappearance was being treated as murder. The police then stopped all night-time searches in order to concentrate on daylight searches in order to maximize forensic opportunities.

Prayers were said in a special church service for April Jones on 7th October 2012 as mountain rescuers ended their role in the massive search. The people of Machynlleth, sorrow etched on their faces, marched silently through the town in an emotional tribute to April. More than 1,000 people gathered to show their support for the missing 5-year-old's family.

On 8th October, Bridger stood in the dock accused of the murder of the little girl. Two further charges were read out accusing him of abducting April on 1st October and intending to pervert the course of justice by the unlawful disposal and concealment of her body up to 3rd October. Earlier, an angry crowd yelled abuse as he was driven in a white police van to Aberystwyth Magistrates' Court. Meanwhile, police confirmed that they were preparing for the fact that April might never be found. Bridger was remanded in custody to appear in court again the following day. (He was remanded in custody pending a further hearing to take place on 11th January 2013.)

At 7pm on Monday 8th October, exactly a week after April was kidnapped, her parents led a moving tribute to their little girl by releasing the first of hundreds of Chinese lanterns and pink balloons alongside their neighbours and the people of Machynlleth.

By 11th October, Prince William and his colleagues from RAF Valley in Anglesey were on standby to help find the body of April Jones. The hunt for the child was not scaled down and was expected to last at least two more weeks at this time. Meanwhile, Coral and Paul Jones were tattooed with pink ribbons, their symbol of hope for their daughter, and were comforted that so many other people also opted to have the tattoos. Ink artist, Rob Williams, had been inundated with people wanting the tattoos in order to show their support. Mr Williams charged £35 per tattoo and donated all proceeds to April's fund, which had so far raised £20,000.

On 22nd October, the police force searching for missing April investigated another attempted child abduction. Detectives were hunting for a man in a white van who grabbed a 9-year-old boy's arm on his way to school. The youngster wriggled free and escaped in the village of Llandybie, Carmarthenshire, 70 miles from Machynlleth. However, police were not linking the two cases. At the end of October 2012, police confirmed that they would not stop searching for April until "we are satisfied we have done all that we can".